1977

ok may be kept

FOURTEEN DAYS

Aspects of modern sociology

Social processes

General Editors

John Barron Mays
Eleanor Rathbone Professor of Sociology, University of Liverpool

Maurice Craft
Senior Lecturer in Education, University of Exeter

Dedicated to my parents

Social control

C. Ken Watkins, BA (Oxon)

Lecturer in Sociology
University of Leeds

Longman
London and New York

Longman Group Limited
Burnt Mill
Harlow
Essex CM20 2JE

*Associated companies, branches and representatives
throughout the world*

Distributed in the United States by Longman Inc., New York

First published 1975

ISBN 0 582 48713 7 cased
ISBN 0 582 48714 5 paper

Set in IBM Century, 10 on 12pt

L.C.# 76 - 350948

*Printed in Great Britain by
Lowe & Brydone (Printers) Ltd, Thetford, Norfolk*

301. 15
N336

Contents

78790

Editors' Preface

The first series in Longman's *Aspects of Modern Sociology* library was concerned with the social structure of modern Britain, and was intended for students following professional and other courses in universities, polytechnics, colleges of education, and elsewhere in further and higher education, as well as for those members of a wider public wishing to pursue an interest in the nature and structure of British society.

A further series set out to examine the history, aims, techniques and limitations of social research; this third series is concerned with a number of fundamental social processes. The presentation is basically analytical, but each title will also seek to embody a particular viewpoint. It is hoped that these very relevant introductory texts will also prove to be of interest to a wider, lay readership as well as to students in higher education.

JOHN BARRON MAYS
MAURICE CRAFT

Acknowledgements

The writer has, of course, accumulated a great number of debts to past teachers, to colleagues and to students.

In particular; Professor Zygmunt Bauman provided both practical help and encouragement, Dennis Warwick prompted the writing of the book and provided continuing encouragement and Ian Varcoe an invaluable critical commentary on early drafts. My continuing discussions with my old friend Dennis Nash must have influenced my ideas in countless, now forgotten, details in addition to the well remembered ones.

I have pleasure too in taking this opportunity to thank Mrs Ruth Sweeney, whose high professional standards must have been occasionally taxed in the preparation of the typescript from what were sometimes very untidy drafts.

My family, finally, coped rather well with the tensions and disruptions of authorship.

The meaning and nature of social control

It is often helpful to approach a new subject from more than one angle. I shall do this in introducing the idea of social control. The very complexity of the idea suggests that this will be helpful, for our concern is to capture an understanding of this idea both in the round, or, as a totality, and in some detail. The two things are of course inseparable, but bringing the most general perspective and some significant detail into relation is by no means always an easy matter. The tactics of presenting overall concern and detail are not necessarily the same.

We shall start by considering the notion of social control in the context of a problem of such generality that, as we shall see it has been argued that no single concept should be required to do so much work. This will give us the general perspective. Immediately after this, with the particular aid of one striking quotation, supplemented by some others, we will start to consider the detail. The particular difference of approach here will be in showing some sensitivity to what I judge to be common associations of the notion of social control which many readers will bring to their first reading of the book. Sociologists purloin commonly used ideas, which they attempt sometimes to use technically, but this does not make the common associations of the idea uninteresting. Indeed, sociological language and the language of everyday life have an unusual and important relationship to one another which makes sociological language somewhat different from the language of the 'hard' sciences like physics and chemistry. This will emerge as we get on with the job of looking at the process of social control.

Social control and social order

The 'problem of social order' is widely regarded as the central 'problem' of sociology. But as my inverted commas will suggest, the sense in which it should be regarded as a problem and the reasons for doing so are at least debatable. Certainly *social control* has been very often employed as a concept which, either uniquely or in combination with others, would resolve this particular problem.

Walter Buckley, in *Sociology and Modern Systems Theory* writes:

> The notion of social control has not had a very successful career in sociology because of difficulties of conceptualisation. It has perhaps most often been made synonymous with sociology itself, *concerned for example with the problem of social order in the broadest sense.* Sometimes it has focused on the conditions for conformity and deviance containment; sometimes on the authority and legitimacy maintaining a given institutional structure. In any case the consensus or equilibrium models of society have worked hand in hand with the 'social control' concept to reinforce one another's weaknesses.[1]

This may seem a distinctly inauspicious start to our consideration of the process. But if we disregard the negative way in which Buckley has expressed his point, his idea of what social control is about can be really rather helpful. He is certainly right in saying that the range of matters with which 'social control' is associated in sociology is broad. It is a fact too that it is clearly associated with the idea of social order. But our next step is to consider what the 'problem of social order' has been taken to be.

The classical formulation of the problem was provided by Thomas Hobbes, the seventeenth-century philosopher. The essence of it is given in the questions: How, if human beings are fundamentally egotistical and self-seeking, is society possible? How is the individual to be restrained from simply grabbing all he can for himself without consideration for his fellows? How are individuals to be obliged to live together in reasonable harmony?

Hobbes's answer to these questions is hardly attractive given the political temper of our times, but quite consistent with this conception of what men are like. His answer too, has notable characteristics that make it of special interest to sociologists. These characteristics are an expression of 'social logic', and, more specifically, an account of how social norms are established.

Hobbes calls the situation in which individuals are free to grab all they can for themselves 'the war of all against all' and 'the state of nature'. The resolution of this condition comes when those who live in the state of nature realise that its intolerable insecurities could be overcome by vesting absolute authority in a single individual. Such an individual—called by Hobbes *Leviathan*, the name that he gave to his book—might by tyrannical, but there are limits to the greed and selfishness of a single man. In addition, given this all-powerful person, there would be some consistency in the rules governing the relationships between individuals. That is, a pattern of norms would be established: Leviathan would determine how people *ought* to behave.[2]

Talcott Parsons is the foremost figure among those whom Buckley is critically characterising as using 'consensus or equilibrium models'. What this amounts to we shall see more clearly in the next section; our present interest in Parsons stems from the fact that he has directly criticised this Hobbesian account of how order is achieved in society. In *The Structure of Social Action*[3] he maintains that Hobbes's proposed solution is a *normative* one. It does not give an account, that is, of how order is in fact achieved in society, but merely some advice on how it *could* be achieved. It amounts merely to a recommendation. In any case, Parsons believes, Hobbes has formulated the question in the wrong way.

For Parsons it is not conceivable that men were ever 'free' in Hobbes's sense of isolated self-seeking individuals, for if they were there would never have been the basis for the formation of society. Hobbes's 'solution' seems to pre-suppose some common conceptions of what would be a better way of life—some values, some behavioural norms. If these men could come together to decide that an all powerful controller was what they needed, they could also agree on something less extreme. But more importantly, Hobbes's solution seems to suggest that they already know how to come to these kinds of arrangement, that they know what it would be to have a contract with one another. But to know such a thing seems to suggest some experience of coopera-tion, so that the very idea of isolated, self-centred individuals is challenged. For Parsons the idea has to be rethought and the proper starting place in his way of thinking is to regard men as normally members of a society which while it con-tinues to exist has a body of norms of behaviour, rules which have moral significance. While the society continues to exist the norms are more or less adequately complied with. Parsons, consequently, has reduced the Hobbesian problem to something much less extensive, though in detail, this is not to say that it may not be very complicated. Accounting for social order has been turned into giving a general account of the way in which the major social values are established and maintained.

Parsons's alternative solution rests heavily on the idea of 'socialisation'. This is a difficult notion, about which there will be much to say. We can approach the idea for the first time and in a preliminary way, most readily through P. H. Landis, a writer on social control whose ideas are simpler and thus more accessible, but who is very similar in content to Parsons. He expresses the essential point in the following distinctly seductive passage:

> Order . . . finds its roots not in some universal laws of nature, not in
> the establishment of recognised external authority [a direct denial,

we see, of Hobbes], but in the social experience of the individual. *Society is orderly because men learn to live so*; it remains orderly until some great revolutionary movement in the social system disturbs the *habit patterns of individuals*. . . . The order exists only in the habits of the individual and in the customs of the social system.[4]

There is in this early statement the basis of reasoning that has been fundamental to a great deal of sociology. These ideas have, however, been made much more refined and sophisticated. The main challenge has been to the idea of habit formation, which suggests a rather simple unthinking repetitive acquisition of behaviour. This could be regarded as an element of a socialisation process but no more than that. A second challenge has come by regarding the formation of the socialisation process as itself something that is in need of investigation.

Social order in this alternative to Hobbes's solution is explained as due to a set of values. These are very general dispositions to behave, inculcated in the individual through a complex socialisation process.

So the Hobbesian solution and its alternative offer us two very broad general conceptions of what social order is and how it is to be achieved. One is an active process, essentially a political or power solution. According to the other the problem seems to solve itself, leaving us simply to study how it happens; the solution is in terms of the society's culture and the 'natural' devices by means of which individuals are inducted into it and moulded by it.

Both 'solutions' have their attractions but neither is good enough on its own. In particular, we can usefully attack the idea that there is always a general solution of the problem of social order such as we are offered in this reasoning. Buckley is right in suggesting that something is lost by regarding a 'consensus' as inevitably being achieved. Such consensus as exists is probably better regarded as a matter of degree, a set of uneasy alliances in which 'power' elements, moral codes, and taken-for-granted patterns of behaviour all play their part.

Reasoning like that of Parsons, in spite of indicating a weakness in Hobbes, short-circuits a lot of the interesting processes that are going on within the society. While socialisation is an absolutely key process in the understanding of social relationships, this way of reasoning throws a much too heavy burden of explanation on the idea. So in its strong formulation, for example, this idea of 'cultural determination' of a social order particularly makes change and dynamic processes in society difficult to understand. As we saw in the short quotation from Landis, social change has to be explained in terms of some great social upheaval which disrupts the society. Once we become committed to the idea of society being based on these fundamental agreed values internal change becomes difficult, if not impossible, to explain. Social control, then, in this way of thinking is simply something residual, a system of fine adjustments which compensate for failures of socialisation. Social order, in its turn, is not fundamentally problematic. It can be explained in terms of the norms of the society, which are in turn the expression of the society's fundamental values. So, if one reasons in this way, the thing to investigate is the *manner* in which social order is achieved. This assumes that it inevitably *is* achieved, for unless this were so the 'society' would cease to exist. It gives primacy to the idea of society and in a sense, defines it. The only concession made to this is that there may be need for 'tidying-up' processes. This is because of the occurrence of 'deviance'—occasional disruptions that have to be put right. Social control then becomes another term for 'the containment of deviance', a residual function which provides a second level of defence of social norms and institutions.

This is one half of the story as posed by Buckley. It is in this way that, as he put it, social control has come to focus on 'deviance containment'. But there are strengths as well as weaknesses in this position.

A strength of Parsons's solution was his unwillingness to separate man from society as Hobbes's formulation of the problem appears to require. Within such reasoning man is accommodated and adjusted rather than controlled. A certain sense of 'social control' that continues to perplex, however, has become curiously lost. Buckley only half succeeds in recapturing this part of the idea in speaking of the way that writers on social control have been concerned with authority and legitimation.

To get a significant feel of what is lost we have to turn either to quite recent work or to some of the older writings on social control. I select a passage from one of the older writers, for its clarity and strength. E. A. Ross, in *Social Control*, first published in 1901, writes:

> In every cluster there are predatory persons—moral idiots or moral lunatics, who can no more put themselves in the place of another, than the beast can enter into the anguish of its prey, or the parasite sympathise with his host.[5]

Strikingly, what this points up are certain possibilities *even within* a strong consensus. Consensus, that is, may be problematic. Predatoriness too is not necessarily an attribute of individuals alone: we may want to think of certain groups in this way. Ross's observation is extreme but it does make us sensitive to what is lost if we adopt Parsons's view of social control. Ross brings home the fact that a range of questions—political questions, in a sense—remain to be answered. Taken to its extreme, an alternative 'answer' to the Hobbesian problem quite properly focuses, as Hobbes himself did, though extremely, on a system of 'political' accommodations. Most notably, this replaces the 'internal' emphasis on value acquisition and its expression in behavioural norms, with an emphasis on 'external' controls, constraints, and accommodations.

These are extreme possibilities then, but two fundamental

components of a discussion of social control—'natural' associations, and 'political' accommodations emerge.

An interesting problem develops through not taking sides too easily. If there is something in each of these positions it is important to see how they may be made to relate to each other.

We have this fundamental agreement with Buckley, then. Discovering a supposed set of values which account for the 'social order' is not good enough. Socialisation, simply backed up by some devices for bringing deviants into line, leaves too many interesting questions unanswered. Strikingly missing is an account of the variations and differences between us, and the relationships of 'give and take'. But let us now look at the topic from our alternative starting point to see how we may make a start on breaking up this subject into some more manageable parts.

Common associations and academic definitions of 'social control'

In sociology no one ever quite starts from 'square one'. Sociology is, truly enough, an academic subject, and as such it sometimes formulates questions which are by no means evidently related to our everyday lives and commonsense understandings. Nonetheless, as members of a society, all of us have a 'sociology' of a kind; indeed on reflection we may find that we have more than one; we have different sociologies for different occasions.

In one sense, a sociology can be simply regarded as our means of 'getting by' in our day-to-day relationships with others, what we know 'in our bones' in the most familiar and commonplace of our relationships. But there is also perhaps a difficult kind of sociology that we sometimes have to struggle to articulate and about which we may find ourselves sadly wrong. This is the sociology of situations which are strange or unexpected, but which we have somehow to cope with, nonetheless; even faced with a strange culture and possibly a language that we do not know, we will probably be able to make some fairly astute guesses about 'how things operate'. So clearly is this the case that sociologists must, indeed, take everyday understandings very much into account when formulating their own analyses. And this cannot exclude the 'everyday understandings' like these latter ones, about which the sociologist, having reflected rather more and having brought to bear a battery of abstract concepts in order to meet the needs of classification and explanation, may with some justification regard himself as rather better informed than the 'layman'.

Both in depth and in breadth, the sociologist ought to be able to regard himself as having something to offer to the non-sociologist. We can easily see why this should be so. The 'everyday sociology' that I distinguished as one of two in an unspecified battery of 'sociologies' (the one which is 'in the bones') is there because it does not need to be anywhere else'. It does not need to be spelt out. Its basis is day-to-day reinforcement; since we 'get by' we know it works and so we do not need to reflect on it. But this leaves open a nice range of questions for sociologists: What is this taken-for-granted reality really like? How does it work? How and why does it change? Why are people sometimes wrong, even in their interpretation of the most common experiences? It may be puzzling in depth precisely because it *is* taken for granted.

The second situation is one in which more self-evidently the sociologist should have something of interest to say. Particularly where unusual cultures are concerned we are all humble enough to presume that the fashion in which they work may well be rather different from our own. Sometimes they are self-evidently different. But if we pursue this point we will fairly quickly be ready to concede that even in our own society, given its large-scale and complex structure, there are probably many groups which operate differently from ourselves. And this leads us straight to the problem of whether and how these different groups are related.

The first part of this question seems to answer itself; the very idea of a society seems to suggest some interrelations between the parts, some coordination of activities. We need not concede that it is a particularly tidy coordination, or conceive society as some kind of 'seamless web' of interrelated activities. We need not, either, commit ourselves to the idea that this is only *one* question. It may be, we shall see as we proceed, that this matter of coordination of activities constitutes a set of questions, rather than a single one. The very conception of a sociology of the 'intimate', face-to-face relationship, and one more nearly concerned with abstract, distant relationships and their interconnection, already suggest that there are at least two questions about social control and consequently a further question about the relationship between these two.

These are commonsense conceptions of the notion of social control. In part, indeed, they are ideas in our culture. These commonsense ideas of social control are unlikely to be homogeneous, so we cannot rely on them being precise or (and this is an aspect of the same thing) meaning the same to everyone. But a way of perhaps teasing out some preconceptions about social control, and consequently starting from 'where we are at', is to consider some of the academic approaches to the social control concept in the light of what appear to be 'commonsense' considerations. Let us start with one of the most attractively phrased and provocative of these formulations.

Barrington Moore Jnr has written, in *Social Origins of Dictatorship and Democracy*:

> To maintain and transmit a value system human beings are punched, bullied, sent to jail, thrown into concentration camps, cajoled, bribed, made into heroes, encouraged to read newspapers, stood up against a wall and shot, and sometimes even taught sociology.[6]

Our immediate 'commonsense' response might well be to challenge the propriety of some of these techniques. We do not associate punching and bullying with legitimate forms of social control. Such techniques seem more evidently and appropriately to belong to informal or unofficial associations, such as boys' gangs, perhaps. Alternatively, they might be regarded simply as random devices by means of which certain people get their own way, and because of their randomness be inappropriately considered as falling within the rubric of social control, which seems to be concerned with structured social realities, realities which fall into ordered and consistent patterns. There are a number of points here which we will look at one at a time.

First, assuming that no one will deny having some conceptions of 'propriety', we must ask whence these are derived. A moment's reflection suggests that these conceptions of 'propriety' are grounded in something like the values which Moore regards as being maintained and transmitted by the social control techniques or devices which he has spelt out for us. But clearly we must not confuse the 'proprieties' that we bring as judgments of acceptable modes of relationship in our own society with the judgments of acceptability that might be current in other societies or among other groups. Indeed, I shall insist that we need to go further than this, and be prepared from time to time to suspend judgment about the rights and wrongs even of our own society's practices and those of groups of which we are clearly members. Failing this, we do something that is perhaps similar to sociological reasoning, but which should be distinguished from it.

Second, although we may naturally regard social control as having particular reference to certain established social agencies—the police, the courts, 'bureaucracy' in the shape of governmental and local governmental agencies, and so on—it is arguable that consideration of these agencies should form a central feature in the study of social control. To some extent this conception of the subject matter is prompted by a conception of 'society' that is too narrow for our purposes. There will be a good deal more to say on this issue later, but for the moment let us note that one of the nuances of the term 'society' does not seem entirely inappropriate when speaking of such things as boys' gangs anyway. Perhaps, for we seem to have moved well beyond what Moore was concerned with, it would serve us better to use a term like 'social structure' or 'social system' to indicate that we want to consider social control not simply in terms of total societies but also in terms of the structured groupings which we may wish to regard as *part* of it, as making it up. In any case, we clearly do not want to be limited by ideas like formality and officialness, which may seem to be associated with certain strong conceptions of society, in setting boundaries to what we regard as being of sociological interest.

Third, we must, I think, take the point that the entirely random event can be of little interest to us. Social control is certainly about the explanation of *patterns* of relationships and ideas and 'pattern' implies some stability. It may be valuable and necessary, however, as we have seen, to regard societies as not necessarily very tidy structures, and consequently we ought not to assume that apparently random or ephemeral events may not be of significance. Indeed to fail to do this may blind us to some of the more significant developments in a society or group, may close our minds to the dynamic nature of society and consequently of its social control processes.

Moore has already given us a good deal of food for thought, but there is more. If agencies like the police were truly the first things brought to mind by the term 'social control' we may recognise that we were concerned essentially with consciously contrived social arrangements, devices intended to be socially functional, clearly directed against deviance and disorder. Moore, however, requires us to think beyond this. His example of 'making someone into a hero', is after all among the techniques that he offers as the means of establishing and maintaining a value system and this prompts several other observations.

First, while there may be certain institutional arrangements for making persons into heroes, they are not of the same order as those functional, organisational arrangements of which we have just been thinking. Such arrangements seem much less conscious and contrived: the natural response of a grateful nation, rather than something institutionalised.

Second, this example is not about containment and control: a reminder that social control need not be a process of deprivation but may involve processes which we may even be *glad* to be subjected to.

Third, 'being made into a hero' is such an odd case that it necessarily provokes the observation that social control may even be concerned with the development and promotion of 'images' or 'models' of rectitude, a vision of some 'ideal' conduct.

The examples, 'being taught sociology' and being encouraged to read newspapers, though they may seem a little tongue-in-cheek, can nonetheless be taken seriously too. They then appear to constitute a kind of middle range of techniques between the coercive at one extreme and the provision of models for emulation at the other. Always provided, that is to say, the newspapers can be induced to print the 'right things', and the sociologists to propound the 'right' doctrines, then these are means by which a continuing commitment to a value system may be ensured; a kind of 'prop' to a system of commitments and ideas that is in fear of failing. In addition it may even introduce some tension among those who have already felt the need to challenge some of the value commitments; inviting them, when confronted with the people and institutions who 'are supposed to know', to think again.

The quotation for Moore, thanks to its explicitness and provocative nature, helps to illuminate some of the detailed implications of a succinct definition of 'social control', like that of A. K. Cohen, and causes us some additional second thoughts. Cohen's definition is much like the intuitive one with which we began. It is simply; 'the prevention and un-making of deviance'.[7] This suggests as a first response, a concern with the formal institutional apparatus of law-making, crime prevention, deterrence and reform. But in case the talk of 'deviance' makes social control seem a rather worthy set of processes, let us remind ourselves both of the distinctly *unacceptable* techniques of maintenance and trans-mission of value systems. Furthermore, Moore's additional example of 'bribery' as a means to this end is oddly disturb-ing. It is so, I think, because we are immediately sensitive to its 'regressive' nature as a technique; it parallels that curious visual phenomenon of endless reflections that we get when mirrors are placed opposite each other. The reason for this is that 'bribery' is paradigm deviance, it can mean nothing other than a deviant act. It is not a term that can stand in for 'reward', for it carries its sense of impropriety with it. But can deviant acts be employed in the control of deviant acts? Clearly, bribery as a device for unmaking one kind of deviance is used at the cost of making another kind. This suggests that values may not be all of a piece, that they may be ranked, that there may be occasions when a lesser form of deviance (bribery?) would be regarded as a small price to pay for the maintenance of what is regarded as a more important value. And this, too, is a useful reminder, for although once pointed out it is commonplace enough, a blanket term like deviance may tend to obscure this evident point. Another different but related point is appropriately introduced here; the general point that it illustrates is important and will come up again.

While 'bribery' is unarguably a term that applies only to a deviant act, it does not follow that the precisely same range of activities which attract the term 'bribery' at one time and in one place will be similarly labelled at other times and in other places. A certain 'commerce' is possible between the characterisation of specific behaviours as either 'bribery' or 'proper inducement'. We shall see too that a society like our own may be complex enough for significant degrees of internal disagreement as to which behaviour to label in which way, to coexist, with certain groups accepting one form of behaviour, others another, and being tolerant of or plainly indifferent to one another.

While the quotation from Moore was not claimed by him to be a definition of social control, that from Cohen was explicitly so. But Cohen's definition was perhaps a little too succinct for our purposes, so let us turn to a third and final definition, this time of a distinctly complex and sophisticated kind. Talcott Parsons's conception of the process is as

> . . . the obverse of the theory of deviant behaviour tendencies. It is the analysis of those processes in the social system that tend to counteract the deviant tendencies, and of the conditions under which such processes will operate.[8]

It has already been suggested that a term like 'social structure' or 'social system' might serve our purposes better and here, in the quotation from Parsons we find 'social system' employed. Among the reasons he uses this term is to achieve precisely the kind of flexibility we needed. This is a more abstract idea than the idea of 'society' that we most naturally subscribe to. It is intended that 'social system' shall be as applicable to the values and structured activities of a boys' gang, to stay with the original example, as it is to the state's arrangements for controlling criminal activity. The relationship to 'values', the term for certain beliefs and ideas which are distinguished from others by virtue of some measure of commitment to them, may well seem more appropriate in application to a boys' gang, where personal relationships are central, than to a formal, bureaucratic set of activities like that of crime control.

It is clear in Parsons's writing and implicit in the short quotation, that he regards 'social systems'—and we must stress what has just been pointed out that this can mean all kinds of social arrangements—as having a tendency to maintain themselves. There are automatic processes or mechanisms

15

which ensure this. This is the idea of equilibrium or stability and we can see fairly readily how the idea of deviance relates to it. To deviate is to move away from equilibrium. 'Social control' consequently, as part of this reasoning, is to be understood as the set of devices which maintain a social order of some kind. And this is something like a natural process.

But now if we set Parsons and Moore side by side we have a strong illustration of the difference between positions on 'social control' that we noticed in the first section. 'Naturalness', is a part of social control for Parsons, as against the implication in Moore of something that comes near at least to contrivance and conspiracy. In certain respects, however, they are in agreement. Though in rather different ways and at different levels of abstraction, they are both concerned with the fashion in which *social order* is maintained. This is evident and explicit in Moore but equivocal in Parsons. Parsons speaks in terms of the values of groups and formally concedes the possibility of tension and conflict between those values and the values of a wider society. But the wider society is clearly the all-encompassing reality, whose mechanisms will accommodate these constituent groups. Parsons has presented us with a good deal more than a set of useful ideas by means of which we may go and study social reality. And too, Parsons's values are the values of 'society', not of some group within it. This is the substantial difference between Parsons and Moore. Moore's 'values' which are 'maintained and transmitted' are the 'values' of a quite distinguishable ruling or power group. Parsons seems concerned rather with some kind of social 'legacy', dominant or majority values.

The question arises whether, although it undoubtedly makes for tidiness in the reasoning, we ought to commit ourselves to 'values' in the seemingly substantial form propounded by both these authors. Certainly we are concerned with consistent patterns of behaviour and the fashion in which that behaviour is established and maintained, but it is perhaps arguable that agreement as to 'values' is not necessarily the basic or the firmest ground on which cooperative relationships exist, and that consequently 'social control' is not exclusively about obtaining compliance with them. In particular, we shall see later when considering the ideas of 'labelling' and 'key positions in the social structure', that values, rather than being the substantial things from which social order is constructed, may be better regarded as 'negotiable ideas'. This must remain a somewhat obscure remark at this stage, but it is our careful reservation that people may agree about less than they seem to, especially where their behaviour is taken for granted by them rather than expressed and explained. Let us simply note, for the time being, that in addition to bringing out this first strong point of contention and providing a preliminary discussion of a number of important conceptual distinctions, a further positive point has emerged which is worth further attention.

The universality and relativity of social control

This positive point is an affirmation of the universality and relativity of social control. Let us return to some previous observations. We remarked earlier on the 'impropriety' of some of the techniques suggested by Moore. The term hardly seems strong enough in speaking, for example, of 'torture' as a technique of social control, to add to the equally obnoxious 'use of concentration camps' which provided the original example. On reflection, however, we may find ourselves seeking justifications even for such measures as these, given extreme circumstances, while no doubt, persistently reminding ourselves that such devices would not 'normally' be regarded as acceptable. It is not too difficult to conceive of 'torture' being argued for as acceptable where the lives of a large number of people, among them children perhaps, were thought to be at stake if the measures were not taken.

Historically, in any case, various groups and societies have been much less squeamish (or enlightened, one can choose what seems the more appropriate evaluation here). We may express this as saying that 'values' are relative. Both historically, and more generally among the variety of circumstances that can be distinguished, which is to say interpreted in various ways, there can be a great deal of relativity in what may be regarded as 'legitimate'. Once again, this is a straightforward point when seen in the light of an example. So, it was clearly possible for the officers of the Spanish Inquisition to justify the most appalling acts against their fellow men on the grounds that no temporal pain and anguish could be regarded as of significance when the saving of an individual's immortal soul was at stake, for this would be to compare a moment in time with eternity and a trifling discomfiture with the unspeakable joy of entering God's kingdom. Given such doctrines as these, while we need no more approve of such acts than we did before, they are no longer incomprehensible. We may find it difficult to believe that anyone honestly espoused such 'values' but they were nonetheless promoted and expressed, and even if we prefer to believe in some 'underlying' motivation, clearly these were values to which certain people regarded themselves as adhering, when and if they reflected on their activities.

This example brings out another, related point. 'A value' is an abstract conception and a consequence of this is that if we try hard enough we can derive formulations which seem to encompass any possible kind of behaviour. So we need to beware of formulations such as the expression of concern with, say, 'ultimate welfare'. An expression like 'ultimate' is a danger signal anyway. We can see that the expressed value of a concern with the individual's ultimate welfare readily fits the example we have just considered and can even encompass putting a man to death 'in his best interest'. Verbal formulations need checking for their 'cash value', what they amount to in practice as inducement or constraint in following recognisable patterns of behaviour.

If we confine ourselves to 'real' values, however, values that are evidently correlated with some kind of behaviour and which eliminate certain possibilities, the relativity of values will be clear. This is only one of a complex of relativities to be confronted. We must not, for instance, confuse the acceptability of certain types of social control technique with their effectiveness. Effectiveness too is a relative matter but one of a different kind. A further type of relativity is that of organisation.

Although different, these distinct and relative aspects of social control are not, for that reason unconnected. Their relationship may indeed be very complex. This much, however, can be said; values clearly condition the range of acceptable techniques; the available knowledge may indeed suggest a range of techniques and organisation that will prove quite unacceptable on other grounds. A current example of social control technique that is available but distinctly disapproved is the range of devices called 'sensory deprivation', revealed by recent psychological research in trying to determine human tolerance levels. Another example, this time at the level of organisation, is that some societies are subjected to very considerable constraints on the acceptable levels of secrecy and discipline which they can impose on their members. Consequently there are constraints on the organisational structure of secret police and similar formations.

This is an appropriate place to remind ourselves too of the relativities of different kinds of groups or relationships. These range from the small-scale and most intimate relationship to the largest and most remote institutions with which we are associated, perhaps some vast bureaucratic commercial or industrial enterprise for which we work. We saw how, to accommodate this kind of variation, the notions of 'social structure' and 'social system' were more appropriate to our needs. Social control, we shall argue, operates at all kinds of levels, not simply at the level of total societies or nation states.

There is, then, a complex weave of interrelated factors in the understanding of social control, but the last remark begins to illuminate the sense in which 'social control' must also be regarded as a universal characteristic. The heading of this section may indeed have seemed paradoxical, but expressly implied in the comparison of Moore and Parsons earlier, in whatever other respects they differed, was the 'fundamentality' of social control.

We can supplement that discussion by simply noting how difficult it would be to conceive, in the light of social control as we have so far developed our understanding of the idea, of any kind of social relationship except the most ephemeral in which some form of control was not operative. The ephemeral relations we may want to exclude as not being in some sense truly 'social'. Particularly, if we take seriously the points just made about the relativity of values and techniques, social control techniques need not be notably unpleasant nor need they be regarded as unusual. They may be built in to the very structure of social relationships of the most varied kind, and at very different levels. Intuitively it was reasonable to regard social control as a kind of natural condition. We might, alternatively, and rather more academically, express this by saying that social control is entailed in the very definition of 'the social'. Either way, in paraphrase, we are saying that social control is a *universal* in society.

These are the two positive points we want specially to note at this stage: the immense relativity of social control, in the several dimensions we have touched on (and indeed others), and its universality in society.

Social control as the interplay of legitimation and solidarity

By both the routes we have travelled we come to a concern with both large-scale and small-scale relationships and their interconnections. What is of central concern is who aligns with whom, why these alignments are as they are, who or what they may be in tension with, and what the conditions of the maintenance and breakdown of these relationships are.

I hope it will be clear now why there will be comparatively little more to say about the more evident devices and agencies of control like the police. They fit in, it will become clear, to a much more general and abstract picture; they are the surface phenomena of a very complex reality into which they slot in a perhaps not altogether expected way.

We want to accommodate both Hobbes's realisation that there are certain tensions between people and groups that have to be resolved, something that becomes a political tension when there is some awareness of differences of interest and view, and the conception of a society as a set of relationships which are natural, or normatively guided, and deviance from which is the puzzling factor. Our key concepts for the understanding of these problems are legitimation and solidarity.

The bias is towards the study of social control as the 'problem of social order'—Hobbes's problem but differently stated and treated. We shall understand this not as a 'social problem' as deviance is so often regarded, but as a socio-logical problem—an interest in how such order as we discover in societies is in fact achieved.

Scale of society:
social control and solidarity

The idea of the 'social'

Like so many of the basic concepts of sociology, that of the 'social' is not defined in a straightforward or singular way. We can readily see why this is so, for it is cognate with the notion of sociology, which as 'the study of the social' serves, like the notion of social control to mark out an area for study which is characterised but not tightly defined. Sociology's own findings, in this way, come to be embodied in our conception of what sociology is.

Part of the foundation already laid, as far as most sociologists are concerned, in characterising the 'social' has been done classically by a founding father of the discipline, Max Weber, some of whose many other contributions to sociological thought we will also exploit. The particular characteristic of the social which was stressed in Weber's formal definition was the very special relationship of the 'social' to individual persons, to their attitudes and beliefs, their ways of 'seeing' and interpreting the world in which they live, their subjectivity. This is important because ways of seeing condition the manner in which people respond to the world. These 'ways of seeing' furthermore should not be regarded simply as a reference to the social world. The object world, the world of things, is also a symbolic world, a humanly interpreted world. We cope with the physical world, most of us anyway, without being what a physicist would regard as 'literate'. The physicist, in any case, responds much like the rest of us, outside his laboratory, to things around him. Our ways of seeing, especially our ways of seeing social relationships, are important in our everyday affairs, and consequently of some importance to sociological reasoning. So much, indeed was implied in early remarks on the need of sociologists to take 'understandings' into account.

Ways of seeing, we need to add here, and this will become evident as we proceed, do not exclude ways of feeling, and it is by no means clear that one approach is more fundamental than the other in determining our response to the world.[1]

Weber defined social action as 'that action which, by virtue of the subjective meaning attached to it by the acting individual (or individuals) . . . takes account of the behaviour of others and is thereby oriented in its course'.[2] This definition is important first because it stresses the 'subjective' realities in social relationships, the ideas, values, attitudes, opinions and so on, of persons. Second, it stimulates reflection on the various ways, clearly of great complexity, in which such relationships may be 'oriented'. How, that is, people relate to one another. One might perhaps call this an understanding of how people locate themselves in social space. It is at least arguable (and, indeed self-evident as an empirical fact, once pointed out) that there are a great variety of forms of relationships between persons. And clearly one of the bases of such differences is a different emotional relationship. This is evident enough at the personal level where our experience of relationships extend over a spectrum from indifference to deepest love.

Notice that even indifference does not exclude the relationship as a social one. For, even in Weber's tightly defined sense the only requirement is that it will be taken into account that other persons will react in some way. Even though the reaction may be passive (for example, the stored up memory of an event, used as the basis of a later response) it *is* both a reaction *and social*. To press this point further, it

23

may seem strange, but one does not cease to be engaged in social activity even when on one's own. Any activity which is oriented to others and consequently takes them into account is social. Consequently many solitary activities are social in this sense.

Both at the personal and the group levels, however, we do distinguish between different degrees of emotional commitment to the relationship, or to use a more technical term which can save us from certain ambiguities, different degrees of 'affective' commitment.

In part this difference between kinds of relationship can be captured by distinguishing a social from a so*cie*tal relationship. This is not entirely satisfactory as will become clear, but will give us some purchase on a necessary distinction. The preliminary distinction I am attempting to establish here is between 'social' as an involved relationship (even if, as in the example I use, it may be quite ephemeral) and 'so*cie*tal' in the abstract and rather colourless sense, the adjective form of the noun 'society'. An example of the first of these uses is a social occasion, a party perhaps. The second means something like 'belonging to society' or 'a part of society'. A rather subtle difference of feeling exists between these two, which will emerge as we proceed. Some careful qualifications may help in this.

What has just been said clearly depends on a distinction between the emotional responses to situations, but the justification for the comment on the less misleading character of the term 'affective' will be clear if we notice that the example of a party must not lead us into thinking that 'social' necessarily means something enjoyable and pleasing. There is no difficulty in thinking of examples of social occasions which are the very opposite of this. The sad coming together of the bereaved after a funeral will serve as a type case to make this point; it is a distinctly emotional or affective situation, nonetheless.

We must avoid too, the inference that emotional associa-

tion should commit us to approval of the social and antagonism to the societal relationship. The terms are not being
differentiated on the basis of promotion of one or the other.
On the contrary, we shall see that there is a certain absurdity
(one that may nonetheless be exploited by certain groups) in
demanding of 'society' in certain of its aspects a form of
relationship that it is quite inappropriate to anticipate and
which we would not necessarily find tolerable, let alone
attractive, if we were indeed subjected to it. A good deal of
recent writing, calling for a return to a simpler, more 'convivial'[3] state, may be guilty of rather simple sociological
ineptitude in this regard. But our concern at present is with
exploration of the variety of different social structures and
their implications for social control and we must not let this
debate distract us. We will be better placed to make some
kind of judgment on it at a later point, and can indeed bring
some useful points to bear on that discussion in the next
section.

The distinction being made here is not unlike a distinction
between primary and secondary group relationships, but
there are two implications of this distinction to which we do
not wish to commit ourselves. The first of these is the implication of stable and permanent structural relationships
which, for example, makes the family the most cited example
of the primary relationship. Our example of the party as
'social' was intended to avoid this implication, for it is not
intended that ephemeral relationships should be denied as
being social. The second is the idea of fundamentality. Once
again, the family is used as the standard example of this
primary quality. Fundamentality usually has a twofold
implication. First, it supposedly serves the interests and needs
of the persons who are part of it; second, it is often regarded
as a functionally necessary part of a society; a basic 'building
block' of any conceivable society is the popular way of
putting it. This latter aspect of the notion of 'primariness'
tends thus to obscure the distinction that we are trying to

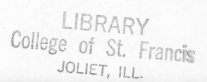

make here, for if it is basic to society it could hardly be more societal.

The pre-reflective feeling that the social is emotionally closer to us, is however an idea that we want to hang on to strongly, for it is truly significant. If we reassociate the two ideas of the social and the societal with the idea of control it will become clear why this is so. *Social* control—making the distinction—looks to be a distinctly intimate sort of affair. We may even want to question whether anything properly to be called 'control' is operating at all in many of the cases that may come most readily to mind. If we stick to the example of the party we may want to maintain that the kinds of party we personally attend are so marked by good manners and friendliness that the very idea of control is completely out of place. In particular, if there is no misbehaviour the question of control clearly does not seem to arise. But I think by now we see this as a distinctly ingenuous response. Certainly it is not to be understood as saying that the party is *un*controlled but, on the contrary, to maintain that it is so well controlled that there is rarely need for any active intervention or restraint of the behaviour. Consequently the control may be quite properly regarded as still operative in these circumstances but to be control of a different order. Among the characteristics of such relationships seem to be a special kind of immediacy of awareness, a non-reflective quality about behaviour. It may all seem distinctly spontaneous too, though this, we shall see later, may be something of an illusion. The voluntary characteristic of the relationship is clearly among its most notable features, and this is perhaps not unassociated with the informality of the control mechanisms.

Certainly, too this last characteristic seems to provide for the strongest distinction, for 'formality' seems to relate very strongly to the forms of societal control, which lack the intimacy associated with the face-to-face and substantially voluntary kinds of relationship. In these latter we can much more readily conceive ourselves as being involved in roles or parts, as against what we more readily regard as being 'ourselves' in the other form of relationship.

The observations we have made on this distinction between social and societal suggest that in spite of the choice of what might reasonably have been first regarded as an ephemeral and comparatively unimportant example in the selection of the party, the social relationship of this kind, or something comparable to it, may be distinctly important, may indeed be more basic as a social formation than the more formal ones with which we have contrasted them. What we may recognise in this is the beginnings or evolution or alternatively the celebration and reaffirmation of *solidarity*. If it is the first of these then we may recognise the possibility of evolution of the association and relationships into others which may become formalised but which whether they do so or not, may be anything but ephemeral.

The source which suggested the party as an appropriate example, is the work of another of the founding fathers of sociology, Emile Durkheim. His work on solidarity is also seminal to our discussion. Durkheim suggested that great gatherings and celebrations of tribesmen might serve the purpose of individual reaffirmation of commitment to others and re-establishment of their way-of-life. We may be going further, however, in suggesting this kind of relationship as a possible *generating* mechanism for more stable societal structures.

We selected from among a number of possibilities a certain intimacy of relationships, a non-reflective quality in the relationships, and informality. Whether these characteristics are to be regarded as cause or effect, how they are related to one another and how they relate to other significant social factors remains somewhat puzzling. Their significance for differences in social control is *beginning* to emerge and by the end of this chapter we will be in a position to suggest why a quite distinguishable subset of ways of developing and

27

maintaining a social order can be associated with such characteristics as these, and indeed why they may be regarded as having wide range significance. But there is clearly some connection here with social scale, either the size of the society at large or the particular social group in which we wish to understand the social control phenomena. We shall see later that what is taken as a failure of social control in modern societies has been thought to be associated most significantly with their scale, which has supposedly played a part at least in the 'impersonality' of large-scale societies, especially industrial ones. We can shortly turn to a discussion of very different types of society and this will help us to get this question of scale into perspective, but before we take this step another distinction will be valuable.

Ideas and 'social reality'; structure and culture

It is both commonplace and self-evident that 'social realities' do not exist simply in our heads. Part of the reason perhaps why the intellectually-minded seem sometimes to be implying this is not unconnected with a deep change in modern industrial societies, which make all of us rather more consciously reflective about everything, including social matters, than were previous generations. However this may be, it is clearly the case that being wrong about the nature of social relationships is quite as common as being wrong about other matters of fact. It may be that if we are powerful or persuasive enough we can change social relationships more nearly to what we want them to be, but if we set aside the distinctly limited utility of 'persuasion' (other than metaphorically) as a technique for changing the physical world, there is no clear distinction in this regard between the physical and the social. In one of its aspects, indeed, social control may be regarded as the set of devices which correct our illusions and misapprehensions about social reality, in a fairly strictly analogous way to that in which physical realities refuse to be denied by providing us with bumps and bruises if we are insistent.

The puzzling feature about the subjective element in social reality prompted by our consideration of Max Weber's definition of social action was the way in which fancy, wishful thinking and the like are to be distinguished from 'genuine', 'realistic', 'true', 'substantial' aspects of social reality (that is, about society in both the social and the societal aspects which we have distinguished). This is a fundamental problem of sociology, to which we should not assume that there is an easy answer. In many areas of social life fantasy and reality do, no doubt, shade into one another imperceptibly. Nonetheless, although a sociological problem in the sense of a problem of formulating the propositions showing the relationships of fantasy and reality in the social world, for most of us and for most of the time this is not a *social problem*. This is because what are to count as sound, realistic, reasonable interpretations of social reality tend to be posed as social problems only in certain rather circumscribed sets of circumstances which, once again, the founding fathers of the discipline have gone a long way in indicating for us. The fact of these problems being exceptional for most of us is an alternative way of making the point made earlier, that we all have a 'sociology' by means of which we 'get by' in our day-to-day affairs. As we shall see later, we sometimes get caught out, but we do not live in an undefined social world, or (for this is a corollary of this last point) one that we can adjust and amend simply in accordance with our wishes.

A shorthand way of making this straightforward but fundamental point is to say that there is a social structure, something not independent of human minds and wills, but not clearly manipulable. But the ideas need not be distinguished from time to time and for certain purposes from this structure; for certain *analytical* purposes we may want to separate them.

An analytical distinction is to be understood, let us be

clear, as a distinction that we make for the purposes of reasoning. It is an aid to thought, not a claim as to what the true elements are into which the world is naturally divided. This distinction between social structure and ideas is to be understood as being like the much more familiar distinction between mind and body. When we speak of the latter we have no illusions about the inseparable nature of mind and body in reality, we take them to be different aspects of the same total reality, the person. And similarly, 'ideas about social reality' and the social reality itself are so intimately related to one another as to be, in some final analysis inseparable.

But 'ideas about social reality' is an ungainly and unmanageable phrase and one that it is easy to replace with something more acceptable. The alternative possibility is, like so many sociological terms, not without difficulties, for it tends to be used with somewhat different meaning by various authors. Provided we are careful to be as nearly as possible consistent in usage, and make a point of noticing variations, the word 'culture' serves well enough as referring essentially to this mental or ideational aspect of social reality. Among such ideas will be many which have gained some kind of permanence and stability among certain groups and even throughout an entire society. The contents of 'culture' so understood will include the many ideologies that may be available. These are the more or less complex and coherent reasonings about the nature of societies in general, offering the groups which subscribe to them the means of explaining or 'explaining away' particular social realities and especially those realities associated with power relationships. Alternatively an ideology may serve as the conception of a *possible* social reality which provides a basis for criticism of the society in which one lives or of others of which one has some knowledge.

Culture, however, involves rather more than these thought out, comprehensive and fairly coherent bodies of interrelated ideas. It can include many fragmentary, poorly specified beliefs and values as well. Indeed some ideas and attitudes may be so poorly formed and articulated that they can only be regarded as embryonic or emergent.

This culture and social structure distinction will serve us in a variety of ways as we proceed, but a word of warning may be necessary. It must be stressed that it is inappropriate and misleading, although 'social structure' is in a certain limited sense more substantial than 'culture', to think of the first of these as an objective reality, while the second is subjective in some less substantial way. The society 'in our heads' and the society 'out there' which we have to cope with somehow, are aspects of the same thing and not, finally, more or less real than one another.

With the battery of useful distinctions formulated in the last few pages, we can now turn to the discussion of what, following the clues we already have, should now seem an almost self-evident basis of distinction between different forms of society. This is, their *scale*.[4]

The significance of scale

A rich source of illustrative material on the nature of the small-scale society is available in anthropological studies which it is appropriate to consider in connection with different forms of social order. Such studies are of social formations very different in their culture, often in clan and tribal formations, who until recently have been thought of as primitive and uncivilised. Much of this work is associated with a long tradition of sociological reasoning, including that of some of the foremost figures in the discipline, in which the people being studied were regarded as representatives of an early stage in an evolutionary social process, and were taken to reveal a range of clues as to our own way of life in the distant past and to the way in which our own large-scale modern societies have developed. This kind of evolutionism is not now much in favour, though some very sophisticated versions of the basic approach are still in evidence. Such materials are full of presumptions which are usefully examined in attempting to tease out the significance of scale for social control. What they are unarguably is the type case of small-scale societal formations. We thus get a clue to the relationship between social and societal forms of control.

The first hazard is in the use of 'simple' and 'primitive', which seem inescapable as descriptive terms for these kinds of social formation but which carry value-laden overtones which it is distinctly difficult to eradicate. 'Simplicity' and 'primitiveness', for the most part are properly to be thought of as applying merely to the technology of these peoples, which by our standards is rudimentary. In certain respects it may also be appropriate to use the term of their art, though here one must tread warily, for the use of the term may simply be an expression of a prejudice in favour of the artistic conventions of the Western world rather than a genuine comment on the range of techniques and skills available to the group. The notion of simplicity may alternatively express a kind of prejudice in favour of highly structured formal social arrangements and the clearly specified distinctions as to task performance and responsibilities, that we have come to regard as functional and appropriate and to which we sometimes give a particular seal of merit by dubbing the arrangement 'rational'.

But neither in the richness of their culture, in the sense that we distinguished as the total complex of conceptions of reality, social and otherwise, nor in the patterned structures of behaviour which make up their social structure are these societies to be regarded as 'simple'. 'Less complex' may serve as a useful characterisation, but even here one must bear in mind that complexity is in significant part a function of the interests and concerns of the observer.

'Primitive' is, if anything, open to even more fundamental sociological objections, the difficulties in large part stemming from the association of the term with the related nineteenth-century conception of progress. This latter is a complex and ambiguous idea in which formal structural development (an aspect of differentiation in modern sociological terminology), level of technology, and moral and religious advancement are run together and assumed to have a particular relationship to one another. The relationship of this set of ideas to a mixture of colonialism and paternalism is evident. They also provide for a degree of self-satisfaction by placing our own form of society at a point on a kind of historical spectrum along which we have 'advanced' and which makes us morally more knowledgeable and worthy, not merely technologically and structurally more complex. It is as if moral and technical knowledge were of a piece with one another. Notably, it is a very strange kind of 'history' that is being appealed to in this kind of reasoning, for these societies are contemporaneous with the society which is supposedly more 'advanced'. 'Simplicity' in tribal societies, if we find ourselves unable to escape the use of the term, is best and least misleadingly understood in terms of differences in technology, formal organisation and differentiation. The last of these will be given further consideration shortly.

There are other possible responses to this kind of evidence about which we must be forearmed. First, we must beware of an alternative kind of prejudice to the one we have just discussed, in which we see our own form of society as necessarily *worse* and less acceptable than those studied by the anthropologist. This kind of prejudice has a stronger basis in the kind of reasoning which the anthropological materials can be used to support. The idea of 'intimacy' properly associated with the small-scale social grouping can readily evoke this alternative but equally absurd prejudice—a prejudice, incidentally, which has equally powerful and authoritative intellectual antecedents. In this way of thinking the 'primitive' or 'simple' society, once again regarded as sharing this quasihistorical evolutionary continuum with our own society, is regarded as offering the picture of some blissful 'ideal'.

This conception sees the 'primitive' society as a kind of state of grace, a natural mode of living, from which the complex modern industrial society is a decline. The idea is associated with that of 'the noble savage', an imaginary predecessor who is unspoiled by our 'artificial' way of life.

Second, rather more technically but also central to our concern with social control, we need to beware of the presumption that a small-scale total society is immediately comparable with small group intimate social relationships; 'the family' may come most readily to mind. This is a kind of imagery from which the preceding misconception, in part draws what persuasiveness it has. There is something to be learned from the small-scale society but the analogy is by no means straightforward or direct. Notably, the family structure, though it may be rather different to our own, is a *part* of these simpler societies as it is of ours. We shall see that we can learn something as to the significance of scale, but it will now be clear that we must be wary of drawing too easy conclusions and parallels.

By way of a final warning on this, let us also note that having dismissed the large family idea we can fairly readily dismiss the happy family idea too. A quotation from Raymond Firth's delightful introduction to anthropology, *Human Types*, will assist in this:

> [Physical] and biological facts, nutritional urges, blood relationships, age similarity, and common residence give a basis for social ties, and link people together in groups. But such factors can also produce disharmony and conflict; clashes between old and young; quarrels between neighbours; sexual jealousy; bickering over inheritance; opposition to economic wants.[5]

'Simple' societies thus are not free of the tensions, problems and difficulties that we experience. This is an important quotation for us, for we shall see that it comes near to characterising 'solidarity', which has had passing mention but which we have soon to develop as one of our key ideas. Quarrels and clashes as well as mutual support and togetherness are important too. The valuable and interesting connecting link between small-scale societies and aspects of our more complex ones, we shall see as being the different part that solidarity plays in them. Scale is a fundamental limiting factor in this, in a sense that is now beginning to emerge.

We can now turn to the further consideration of *differentiation* as a major basis of distinction between these complex industrial societies. It is an important idea for us in being closely related to the form and nature of social control in the different societies. *Lack* of differentiation is perhaps most readily explained. This means a kind of running together and confusion of functionally distinct and separate aspects of the society. The simplest illustration is probably that of the cultural differentiation established in societies like our own between morality and the law. This has its structural correlates; and notably while moral and legal factors often overlap in some measure we do not confuse the priest with the judge. At a somewhat different level, two quite separate and independent institutional complexes, the Church and the Law, exist as the institutions within which the distinctive roles of the priest and the judge are played. Differentiation thus takes place at a number of related levels, which are quite inseparable, the priest (though not of course the 'holy man' or the prophet) being unthinkable without the Church and the solicitor and barrister being unthinkable without the legal system. Institutional differentiation and role differentiation, to put it technically, are clearly related to one another. The distinction being made is one of specialisation of roles and functions and of the accompanying associated ideas, which are not to be found in the tribal societies.

Clearly, too, differentiation is associated with technological complexity. With the expansion of the variety of skills there is an expansion of the variety of skilled roles in the society, and this of course is inevitable because tautologous; it is the alternative expression of the same fact.

Let us now notice another aspect of the tribal form of

society which, though it may be properly regarded as simple in the sense that we have carefully distinguished, is not properly to be regarded as small-scale in terms simply of the numbers of individuals who are members of the tribe. Clearly, they are smaller than industrial nation states, but their membership may well consist of thousands of individuals. Their active relationships are not small in number and thus are not simple in that sense. But the *patterns* of ideas (beliefs, attitudes, and the like) and the *patterns* of activity are fewer in number and complexity. This is illustrated most readily in terms of industry, the means by which a living is gained. The Nuer, to take a specific example of a people who have been studied in depth by the famous anthropologist, E. E. Evans-Pritchard,[6] are a herding people whose economy centres round a few cattle. Even though this has a degree of complexity, it is not comparable to the complexity of work roles and relationships in industrial society even on the smallest scale. Furthermore, the true unit of normal interaction is not the tribe but either the village unit or the nomadic group, and what is more nearly the point in terms of scale is the repetition of *patterns* and idea structures among the members of the tribe. Durkheim, to whose work we must shortly turn in considering the nature of solidarity in different kinds of society, made use of a term with some affinity to the idea that we need to express here, in speaking of 'segmental' structure of societies. In our somewhat modified sense we can regard the village community or the nomadic group as the segment of the tribal society. As we shall see, what is particularly important for our discussion is that the large-scale industrial society cannot be regarded as segmentary in the same fashion. This is important, consistently with Durkheim's reasoning, in that different possibilities for solidarity, and consequently differences in the nature of social control are implied.

An ambiguity in the use of the notion of society is evident here. Notice that there are two perfectly proper senses in which the term is being used. Abstractly, we simply mean any complex patterns of relationship and ideas which we have distinguished as characteristic of the tribe, nation, or whatever social form we are discussing. Substantively, we will be considering some actual group of human beings in relationship to one another. We may therefore speak of the society (abstract sense) being 'represented' in the tribal society by any one of its segments; and the segments notably are 'total', the whole pattern of life of the individual is worked out within them. This is quite unlike the pattern of life of the individual in a large-scale society (abstract sense) who is involved in a much more complex set of interrelationships, whose way of life will depend on countless people he will never meet, performing tasks of which he may have no appreciation or understanding whatever, and even thinking thoughts and having attitudes and beliefs entirely 'foreign' to him. He is not part of a way of life that is a straightforward repeat pattern of the way of life of the members of another segment and which is the basis on which we regard them as belonging to the same 'society' (abstract sense). Indeed the pattern of life of the individual in a complex industrial society can be unique (without being in any way eccentric) simply in virtue of the range of possible social structures in which he may play some part. It is these senses of simplicity and complexity that are involved in discussing the relationship between the primitive and the complex forms of society. In the abstract sense we see that we are thinking of the 'model' or 'idea' of the total society, our *image* of the substantive society, the actual relationships between people.

Mass society seems an appropriate term for the polar opposite of the 'simple' society we have just been considering. Once again we have some trouble with the associations which the term may carry, but for our immediate purpose we can use it technically now that we have a background of discussion. Consistently with the remarks concerning the nature of simple societies our own kind of industrial society is first and foremost distinguished by the complexity of its role structure. In the nature of things a great deal of the activity of other persons in our kind of society is 'invisible', not merely in terms of its being undertaken in shops and factories away from our view but more profoundly in terms of our understanding of what other people do. Mass society is immensely specialised.

This has implications for the range of associations and relationships that are possible for us—and this is of course a profound difference from that of the 'anthropological' societies where individuals are known *as such* and what they do is generally understood and appreciated, even where the skills are not shared. Sheer numbers in our kind of society limit the possibilities of personal acquaintanceship, even without the limitations imposed by technical specialism. We manage this kind of situation by entering into a great number of almost pure *role relationships*, and in this respect are again part of a social structure quite unlike that of a tribal group. A lot of our activity is patterned in terms of sets of quite stable expectations in which very little involvement is incurred. We anticipate more or less competent and predictable performance from all kinds of persons with whom we have something like a 'commercial' relationship—and we, in our turn, when in such service roles, perform similarly. A great number of our day-to-day relationships, to put this in a slightly different way, are service and commodity relationships, mostly rather simple patterned relationships like those in which we engage with a shop assistant or bus conductor. We do not need to know one another personally nor to have any significant knowledge of the technicalities of the function the other person is involved in.

This point might be expressed by saying that the simple societies are 'solidaristic' in a way which our kind of society is not and could hardly conceivably be. This has very important implications for the social control process in the different societies. To help us in unravelling the complexities involved we can turn to Emile Durkheim's classic discussion of the problem of solidarity in large-scale industrial society which he developed in *The Division of Labour in Society*.[7]

We have already drawn on ideas about the division of labour in society that were expressed by Durkheim as long ago as 1893. The immediate association of the idea is possibly with industry and commerce in the seemingly endless variety of specialisms developed by industrial and commercial enterprise in their search for more efficient modes of production. Specialism can become so esoteric as to be a source of humour. The following, for example, are among the occupations listed in the Registrar General's Classification: tyre bowler, toggle strainer, whimseyer, whizzerman.

Durkheim was, however, intensely aware that this specialisation and fragmentation of activity extended beyond industry:

> But the division of labour is not peculiar to the economic world; we can observe its growing influence in the most varied fields of society. The political, judicial and administrative functions are growing more and more specialised. It is the same with the aesthetic and scientific functions.[8]

I have expressed much the same point in the preceding paragraphs, using the now more common sociological terminology which expresses it in terms of the complexity of role structure. Although Durkheim used the notion of the complex division of labour in certain 'advanced' societies, in a similar way, it was however rather more committed. The commitment relates to the mode of thinking which we spoke of earlier in which a kind of historical continuity— evolution—connects different kinds of society. Of the division of labour Durkheim remarked that 'since it combines both the productive power and the ability of the workman, it is the necessary condition of development in societies, both intellectual and material development. It is the source of civilisation.'[9] Later, he commits himself to the view that the division of labour can be no less than a significant moral

Social control

force that creates 'in two or more persons a feeling of solidarity'.[10]

The index or objective indicator of different kinds of solidarity Durkheim finds in different kinds of law. This is a clue to the connection in Durkheim among the division of labour, social control, solidarity and the social order. Although we shall not follow him in this, and the relationships we are establishing between these factors in social structure and culture are fundamentally different from those of Durkheim, we must necessarily spell out briefly how he envisaged the relationship between different forms of law and different forms of solidarity. The two fundamental forms of law that Durkheim distinguishes are repressive law and restitutive law. His own characterisations of them are as follows:

> Some consist essentially in suffering, or at least a loss inflicted on the [law-breaker]. They make demands on his fortune or on his honour, or on his life, or on his liberty, and deprive him of something he enjoys. We call them repressive [sanctions]. They constitute penal law. . . . As for the other type it does not necessarily imply suffering for the agent, but consists only of *the return of things as they were.* . . . We must then separate juridical rules into two great classes, accordingly as they have recognised repressive sanctions or only restitutive sanctions.[11]

Associated with the first of these, repressive sanctions, Durkheim calls the first of his two forms of solidarity *mechanical solidarity.* Mechanical solidarity is associated with the so-called primitive societies which we considered in the previous section. It is, according to Durkheim, fundamentally grounded in likeness or similarity between the participants. This likeness and the commitment to it accounts for repressive sanctions, for differences are regarded as offensive. Consistently with what we said earlier, a characteristic of primitive societies is the rudimentary character of the division of labour. Similarity between such peoples is a fundamental characteristic, as we argued; patterns of relationships, range of skills, beliefs, attitudes and so on, are all much

40

less complex and differentiated and consequently much more homogeneous than in a complex modern society.

Durkheim is making a predominantly cultural point (in our definition of this term), speaking about the complex beliefs and attitudes of the society rather than about its structure; indeed his book can be read as a formulation of an important relationship between types of social structure, simple or highly complex division of labour, and the corresponding complex of attitudes and beliefs. To the latter Durkheim gave the distinguishing term *conscience collective*, which is interestingly ambiguous when translated into English, for the French word *conscience* means both 'conscience', linking the idea with morality, and 'consciousness', linking the idea with subjective understanding. Durkheim's usage exploits both senses. Members of societies characterised by mechanical solidarity are governed by very clearly specified penal rules which are harshly sanctioned. *Shared* consciousness can also be regarded as an antithesis to *individual* consciousness, a kind of parallel thought in Durkheim to the antithesis of collective and individual conscience; certainly Durkheim regarded the consciousness of individuality of man in complex modern societies as being a characteristic that was not shared by man in the mechanically solidary 'simple' society. In this sense, the member of this society is more immersed in, more integrally a part of, his society. This is a corollary of the conception of shared common consciousness and conscience. This is brought home strongly in a further quotation from Durkheim:

> There are in us two consciences—one contains states which are personal to each of us and which characterise us, while the states which comprehend the other are common to all society. . . . Although distinct these two consciences are linked one to the other. . . . From this results a solidarity *sui generis* which, born of resemblances, directly links the individual with society.[12]

The translation of *consciences* here might perhaps have been better rendered as 'forms (or modes) of consciousness'.

41

The passage then would more clearly become a comment on the relationship of unique consciousness (awareness of personality) to the ideas and attitudes that are available from the society, the 'culture'. We shall pursue this further when we consider the relationship of self-image to the mechanisms of social control.

The alternative form of solidarity for Durkheim is organic solidarity. As we have already seen, Durkheim associates this form of solidarity with an alternative form of legal sanction, the restitutive sanction. Under this form of law, reinstatement of losses (damages) rather than punishment, is the distinguishing characteristic. The societies characterised by organic solidarity are functionally integrated societies, societies, that is, in which there is a great deal of differentiation of tasks and which are dependent on a relationship, however contrived, of cooperation between these various elements. Common sentiments are less evident in such societies. On this it is again valuable to return to Durkheim. In so doing we must note carefully the ambiguity of his 'conscience' idea.

> In fact it is in the nature of the special tasks to escape the action of the collective conscience, for, in order for a thing to be the object of common sentiments, the first condition is that it be common, that is to say, that it be present in all consciences and that all can represent it in one and the same manner. To be sure, in so far as functions have a certain generality, everybody can have some idea of them. But the more specialised they are the more circumscribed the number of those cognisant of each of them.[13]

Notably 'conscience', understood as consciousness, presents us with the possibility of an individualism in complex societies quite different from and much more highly developed than in the kind of society characterised by mechanical solidarity. Durkheim seems to regard this as a kind of corollary to his reasoning about the nature of collective consciousness, for individuality and collective consciousness are offered as plain alternatives. 'If we have a lively desire to think and act for ourselves, we cannot be strongly inclined to think and act as others do.'[14] We should be suspicious of this, however, for it does *not* follow that the availability of choice necessarily undermines unity; in Durkheim's own terms it simply undermines automatic or mechanical unity.

The second form of solidarity, then, is seen as developing out of a complementarity of differences, a coordination of functionally related specialisms where the only thing comparable to the mechanical solidarity of the simple society is to be found in the common usages of skilled specialists, craftsmen and the like. There is little doubt that Durkheim regarded this second kind of solidarity as being both real and fragile. Its fragility indeed troubled him. For our part, we are entirely justified in questioning in what sense the second form of 'solidarity' is properly to be regarded as such.

What has to be distinguished is the *factual* complementarity of differences from the *recognition* of such complementarities. The complexity of society has many implications; one of these of which Durkheim was distinctly aware, as we have seen, was of difference in consciousness. However important the various roles in the society and their interrelationships may be to us we might simply not *care*. The pluralism to which Durkheim is sensitive allows for both ignorance and indifference, with the consequence that we are provided not with answers but with a whole new range of questions. Among such questions, consistently with Durkheim's functionalist mode of reasoning, might be that of whether we can identify some organisation or some complex of organisations in such societies which serves to maintain a necessarily diffuse awareness of our need for one another's skills and competences. If the answer to this seems self-evident, if, for example, we think we have located such an instrument in the mass media, what may at least be regarded as problematic is the significance of such a diffuse commitment in our day-to-day relationships with one another, for nothing evidently follows from such a diffuse commitment.

There is, it would seem, a relationship here to what we earlier described as societal control, to distinguish what seemed a more intimate control complex. Failing this integrating device, indeed failing its effective performance, the logic of the situation of pluralism and complexity would seem no more clearly to be solidarity and integration than extreme individualism or perhaps group factionalism. But Durkheim can hardly be regarded as having provided the conceptual instrument for the analysis of this. The question of the acceptance of some common conception of the 'rightness' of a social structure we shall see later as being appropriately handled by means of Max Weber's theory of legitimation.

There is a rather different further point which is absolutely central to our discussion, stressing again the need for the distinction between the social (or primary) in social control, and the societal. Given Durkheim's diffuse cultural commitment it is easy enough to concede, in the abstract, that we are dependent on countless specialisms in a society for our wellbeing. But this by no means commits us to any particular individuals. Our recognition, e.g., of the importance of the medical profession is on a quite different level to our commitment to the family doctor. We need not insist that there is no relationship between these two levels, but we must be very aware of the difference between them if we are not to obscure the interesting problem of that relationship.

These remarks emphasise that we must not allow ourselves to be deflected by Durkheim from *our* concern to his. Durkheim's concern was with social order, as a functional constitutive aspect of society. He conceived of society as being of necessity, almost as a defining characteristic, a strongly bound relationship of persons. As we have seen, his sociology involves an equivocation about the nature of that bond, shifting from a moral reality (conscience) to a cognitive reality, one of shared meanings (consciousness). His concern has sometimes got in the way of the development of the notion of social control. In certain respects Durkheim, although helpful in other regards, simply begs the interesting questions. The lessons to be learned from this consideration of his reasoning stem from the useful distinctions that he has helped us to make—and particularly for what I shall maintain is a powerful, evocative and convincing image of mechanical solidarity which, when freed from its association with 'primitive' societies, provides a powerful foundation on which to develop an understanding of solidarity as a fundamentally important form of social control. This is not a new point but one that has either been given the burden of explaining social control in its entirety or been ignored completely, usually in favour of an account of social control which effectively regarded it as a variety of means of coercion.

There is a further and important common factor in both our own and Durkheim's reasoning in the realisation of the significance of *scale* in the understanding of solidarity and social control. Mechanical solidarity, in Durkheim's terms, understood as capturing much of the substance of solidarity in the sense that we are developing, is a phenomenon in which the number of participants and the degree of participation is to be regarded as a distinctly limiting factor.

'Community' as happy medium

The notion of community[15] will come up later for deeper consideration but a few passing comments at this stage may be both an assurance that a point has not been missed and a contribution to continuity.

We have spoken briefly of the small-scale society and the mass society, and the reader might reasonably regard this as dealing with extreme social forms without giving attention to the most common. This would be a reasonable response. The reasons that 'community' gets only a superficial consideration at this stage are, first, because it is the most complex and difficult case, and second, that certain characteristics much more central to the idea than scale of society are involved.

To this point our concern has been simply with scale of society, though it has emerged that solidarity becomes tenuous with the increase in scale. In the next chapter I shall aim to show that the tenuous character of solidarity is associated with the socialisation process. 'Community' is a complex notion and, once again, it is one that has been used in a great variety of distinguishable ways in the literature. In one of the more important and interesting ways for us it has implied a special kind of relationship that exploits the ideas of smallness, frequency of association and an associated socialisation process. The village community serves as example and type case of this. In the most important respects 'community' so regarded is not unlike the small-scale societies we have considered.

'Community' is also a word much used for a quality of association, with the consequence that a term such as 'world community' expressed as an aim, or possibly in reference to certain international institutions or agencies like those of the United Nations Organisation, is quite comprehensible. Perhaps the central matter stressed in this use of the term is a combination of cooperation and concern. We shall consider later some of the implications of the thought of Ferdinand Toennies, one of the principal sources of this usage; the points specially at issue at this stage are the possibility of extension of the term over this very wide spectrum of social relationships and institutions and the implications regarding the quality of the relationships.

Our own stress will be much more nearly a concern with the quality of the relationship which is part of the connotation of this complex idea than with the scale of relationships with which it is associated. It will be clear that two rather different distinctions—which we need not deny may be related but whose relationship we would like to consider rather than simply assume—are intertwined. The focus on community as a quality of relationships is a choice, not a necessity of reasoning or forced upon us by evidence; but it is an informed choice, for the concept appears to lose what is truly of its essence if one denies the way in which it refers to a quality of association. To deny it as a concept which distinguishes a middle scale of relationships from the small-scale and the 'mass' relationship, as our simple example of 'world community' showed, seems not to deny what is of the essence of the idea and allows us to avoid the running together of the distinct characteristics that I have indicated.

The 'scale' of a social group, we have seen, is significant for the form of social control. There is a 'primary group' quality about many of the anthropologists' societies which suggests that the 'solidarity' dimension is all important. As we argued above, however, we must not picture them as overgrown 'happy families'. Indeed, this kind of conception is doubly naïve, for once again, while the family is the paradigm example of the primary group, the idea of the family as necessarily worthy, happy, a model of what a 'good society' would be like, must, to put it mildly, be accepted only with massive qualifications. It is now some considerable time since Leach called it 'the source of all our discontents'[1], but this phrase still has some shock value, and can still prompt heated debate. A generalised presumption about the nature of family life, overlaid by the immensely powerful though perhaps consciously 'dim' memories of the reassurance and support that it afforded when as children we were at our most vulnerable, inclines most of us towards a commitment to our own families, and by extension and generalisation a commitment towards the family structure in general.

This begs many questions of a technical kind, not least the question of the representativeness of our experience or what we take to have been our experience of family life. For the latter is a complex of remembrances and associations not only with immense emotional overlay but which have been subjected to interpretation and reinterpretation as we have developed critical awareness and the conceptual means of formulating our understanding of these relationships.

The common primariness which they share is intimacy—the face-to-face and day-to-day quality of the association. And in this, they both differ from much of our experience in the large-scale industrial societies to which we belong.

Socialisation and solidarity

Readers with some previous grounding in sociology will perhaps be a little surprised that we have come so far with only passing mention of the process of socialisation. Socialisation is often regarded as the virtually exclusive key to the understanding of social order, social control being a residual phenomenon. But here speaking of the small-scale and intimate society where the socialisation process recommends itself almost self-evidently as the key to the understanding of social order may clearly provide a kind of link between the small-scale 'primitive' society, certain aspects of 'community', and, even mass society. We must now give a little deeper consideration to the concept of socialisation.

'Socialisation', like 'social control' in sociology, gets an enormous amount of work to do, and for the same reason. If we deny none of the potential scope of the idea, however, but nonetheless insist on focusing our concern on certain strong aspects of socialisation, its close relationship to solidarity begins to be evident. The major things to be stressed here are the emotional involvement that is part and parcel of the socialisation process, and its links with self-image and identity.

The most succinct characterisation of socialisation is as that complex of processes through which we become social beings. In this aspect the most profound and fundamental application of the idea is to the newborn child, who must set out on a journey of discovery of the culture and social structure into which he has been born. By a prolonged and largely natural process ('natural' in the sense that the participants are

not consciously directing the process) certain ways of thinking and acting which we regard as human and social come to
be adopted by the child. Among these learned techniques and
beliefs ('learned' because they are not inherited or innate) are
some which are so fundamental that the individual can hardly
be regarded as human unless they are somehow imparted and
acquired. This involves processes that may be regarded as
similar to indoctrination, learning, natural adaptation to the
environment; all of these things and others. There is no clear
synonym for the term 'socialisation', and this is the best
possible reason for coining it.

The socialisation process implants not only information, or
what is regarded as information in the given society, but also
attitudes to people, things and ideas; selective responses to
certain kinds of action and beliefs; and basic categories of
understanding and classification in general.

An important aspect of this is in its relationship to the
child's emotions, its sensations of pleasure, fear, and so on.
Its actions provide a variety of responses some of which are
pleasurable and rewarding, others are not. The child is thus
prompted into certain channels of action and discouraged
from adopting others. Since he has as yet no basis for reasoning, the socialisation process itself providing the necessary
fundamental categories that will make this possible, the newborn child can be regarded as an almost purely emotional
creature. We can note a useful parallel here with emerging or
not fully formed social relations, and with some kinds of new
situation which the individual has to confront. The last of
these is the simplest. We are clearly vulnerable and disorien-
tated in some degree when a new situation confronts us; we
have to 'map out' the social 'geography'; this is clearly different in degree from the situation of the child, principally
because we have a lot of basic knowledge about social
relationships. Nonetheless, the emotional tensions and the
problems of discovering new modes of behaviour and
accepted categories of understanding suggest a difference of

degree in adult socialisation situations rather than a difference of type, when they are true accommodating (i.e., joining) or emerging (i.e., creating) relationships. Childhood socialisation is distinguished as *primary* socialisation because of its fundamentality, which is what is at issue in the parallel case. However, in the case of the child a repertoire of actions will be built up, and these actions will have deep emotive or affective associations, being grounded in the emotions of the child rather than in its intellect.

As with the social process, we should be careful to avoid any conclusions about the extent to which the persons in any particular society are subjected to the same techniques of socialisation *or* are inculcated with the same substantive ideas or patterns of behaviour. In other words, the *universality* of the socialisation process does not imply universality of content or technique. It is much more reasonable to anticipate wide differences. It may be possible by investigation to show some of these differences as consistent, for example, between different social classes, different ethnic groupings, different religious associations. In short, the different 'significant others'[2] with whom the child has most frequent or emotionally deepest contact can be an important clue to his pattern of behaviour and beliefs.

Early or primary socialisation sets down patterns of belief and consistent responses to a variety of *social relationships* and these are emotionally charged so as to be felt by the individual as being emotionally right or wrong, proper or improper. But note the stress on 'social relationships'. While these actions and ideas and their emotional association may not be totally unchangeable, they constitute some kind of foundation for later responses to comparable social situations as seen or 'felt' by the individual. With the later development of self-awareness, many of these ideas and responses come to be interpreted and absorbed into the self-image of the individual, his internal picture of what sort of a person he is. With the later development too comes the possibility of rational reflection on the selection of the individual's ideas and actions. It does not follow that the socialisation process is now at an end: it becomes more nearly like adult learning, something (potentially at least) much more under the individual's control. Still not wholly so, if only because of the preconditioning effects of early socialisation. One continues to have experiences that are rewarding and those that are the reverse, and one continues to 'learn' from these—sometimes not—and in this sense the socialisation process continues throughout life. This is additional and supplementary to formal learning and training which, of course, has its socialisation element.

Several of the more evident ways in which socialisation is related to social control are now beginning to emerge. Most notably, perhaps, the manner in which the less extreme of the social control mechanisms can operate. If it can be effectively indicated or merely suggested to us that a present action is inconsistent with what we ourselves regard as a proper and right form of behaviour, then there is a likelihood that the behaviour will be amended. Similarly (a very closely related phenomenon) if an action can be indicated or implied as being 'unlike you', an appeal can be made to one's self-image, and once again an adjustment may be provoked.

A whole range of techniques can readily be compiled which make use of hints, suggestions and indications that we are not doing what we know to be right. Whatever the logic of the situation intimations of 'incorrectness' by our own standards, or inconsistency with our own self-image are likely to be responded to differently and especially to call forth a different emotional response than would an order or even advice. Any tendency to regard socialisation and social control as some kind of opposites is revealed as a dangerously misleading simplification. One must therefore avoid the common usage of the term 'unsocialised', as a simple expression of disapproval for particular behaviour, with the intimation that the individual 'hasn't been brought up right'.

There is no challenge here, of course, to the right to disapprove. What is objectionable in this usage is the usual
failure to recognise the universality of socialisation, a process
which we can only fail to receive by not having association
with other human beings, in the fashion of Romulus and
Remus, the standard example of non-socialised or feral
children. It follows that social control is not a straightforward replacement for socialisation, some complementary
measure that has to be applied to the 'unsocialised'. In a very
guarded way we may speak of 'defective socialisation', but
the warrant for this is the previous establishment of the fact
that an individual, first, by some standards belongs to a
particular social class or group; and second, that this group
has clear patterns of behaviour to which the individual does
not adhere. It is as if he *ought* to know better, but does not.
It is this kind of situation that is envisaged in the objectionable use of 'unsocialised'. The unwarranted assumption is
that of *universally correct* patterns of behaviour, which is
quite different from the universality of the process.

It will be less misleading if we regard socialisation and
social control as shading into one another in a number of
circumstances. But equally consistent with what we have
discovered is that different socialisation contents will distinctly *imply* social control needs in complex societies. There
will be genuine differences of behaviour and belief which are
strongly established and may from time to time create
tensions and conflict situations that have somehow to be
accommodated. This is a problem of social control and the
beginnings of a clue as to how the social and the soci*etal* are
interrelated. As with earlier examples it indicates the many
levels at which the notion of social control operates and
hence the variety of techniques and agencies appropriate to
it. It has, too, an increasing significance as complexities of
society and 'scale', in the minimal sense of the numbers
involved in the process of interrelationships, increase.

Although we have not confined ourselves to it exclusively,

our principle concern in describing the socialisation process has been with 'primary' socialisation. The reason for this is clear enough: the process is easier to explain in its 'primary' form, for it is clearer and tidier, and in certain important respects fairly self-evident. Not without cause, however, it has been complained that 'socialisation' explains too much. This appears especially to be the case if we attempt to extend it beyond the early phase. Dennis Wrong argues thus:

> What has happened is that internalisation has imperceptibly been equated with 'learning', or even with 'habit-formation' in the simplest sense. Thus when a norm is said to have been 'internalised' by an individual, what is frequently meant is that he habitually affirms it and conforms to it in his conduct. The whole stress on inner conflict, on the tension between powerful impulses and super-ego controls, the behavioural outcome of which cannot be prejudged, drops out of the picture.[3]

We may read the reference to 'superego controls' as meaning 'conscience' without distorting the argument in any way, and Wrong as being concerned to distinguish between certain very basic characteristics of man which 'conscience' through the internalisation process plays a significant part in controlling. This, and the talk of 'internalisation' is a different mode of expression consistent with the explanation of socialisation that I have just given, and with arguments which we considered in chapter 2. (See particularly pp. 24—7.)

The alternative expression is useful, in underscoring certain features of socialisation process that may not have been sufficiently stressed. Thus, it is clear in what precedes that we need to regard socialisation in its significance for personality formation very seriously indeed. Early socialisation is, indeed, an important explanatory concept for the understanding of this, and 'internalisation' a neat term to express this idea of the establishment of the individual's conception of himself. Clearly too, given a built-in conception of this kind, one of the most significant controls over behaviour is conscience or super-ego. This is distinctly not to say that the individual's problems of how to behave are finally and irrevocably solved, and for a number of reasons. The first, as Wrong has seen, is that 'conscience' can be and frequently is disobeyed. Second, there is a sense in which every problem of behaviour which any of us have to face is unique. This is not a point about the complexity of our kind of society, though this complexity may present us with a wide range of situations that cannot occur in a 'simpler' society. It is rather a question about how we classify and order our experiences; what we *count* as similar questions or problems and consequently what we regard as appropriate answers or responses to them, if indeed we can provide any. The third reason is that it is not clear that one learns 'normative' responses independently of learning the 'normative' categories of person to which the normative responses attach. The emotionality which is such a central matter in the early socialisation process very rapidly, it seems, attaches to persons. So no one anticipates, even from quite young children, the precise response to what is notionally the same action performed by mother or father, when it is performed by a stranger. Early socialisation, it seems, is more plausibly context specific in the responses it evokes, than 'normative' in the sense of patterned in terms of universal responses to the 'same' situations or acts. This perhaps draws what plausibility it has from the evident patterning of pain-avoidance and pleasure-seeking activity, but the first is not usefully to be regarded as normative activity and the second is problematically so.

While we want to retain the explanatory power of the 'socialisation' concept in assisting us to understand how personality structure may be built up and in indicating some of the most subtle and all-pervasive of the social control devices, it should be clear that there are a great number of unspecified relativities involved in this. Furthermore, socialisation is clearly much more powerful an idea in terms of our notion of the *social* than it is in terms of the *societal*. There are clearly implications for the relation of socialisation and solidarity.

Beyond early socialisation, as we have already remarked, the process comes to be much more nearly adequately described as a 'learning' process. On occasions, as with an apprentice learning a trade, it is consciously directed, though it does not follow that what the apprentice learns is only what he is 'taught'. For example, if he is an industrial apprentice he is likely to assimilate a great deal about the broadly accepted relationships between management and men in his factory and between various craftsmen and workers of different status. Acceptance of such relations may become normative to a degree, to the extent that they are regarded as the 'right' way of behaving and become imbued in some measure with *moral* force. To stick with the example, the apprentice may rapidly come to regard the borrowing of workmates' tools not merely as not the thing to do, but as distinctly an improper thing to do. One can thus properly speak of the 'internalisation' of a rule, but it is distinctly context specific.

As we move away from early socialisation the process becomes in many respects less distinctive, more nearly like a learning process, more conscious and available to manipulation. It is still a process associated with emotional commitment and is, I shall maintain, of the essence of solidarity. But trying to explain too much with the idea of socialisation poaches on certain ideas that are much more satisfactorily conceptualised as part of the process of legitimation. To this process and once again to Weber, for the classical formulation of the notion, we can now turn.

Weber's concept of legitimacy

The essential question which is answered by means of the concept of legitimacy is 'Why does any person or group obey the instructions of any other?' But this is merely the central question posed and answered by the concept of legitimacy. Legitimation can refer as readily to any set of social arrangements that is subject to challenge. Quite generally, it is a reply to the question 'Why should one do things in this way, and not in some other?' But we can come to the more general question most readily by way of the question of justification of relationships of 'authority'. The answer to the first of our questions, and perhaps in part also to the second, is, at the extreme, simply in terms of some kind of self-interest. So, a variety of means of coercion, physical, psychological or, more subtly structural, may be the devices, by which the powerful obtain the necessary minimal cooperation of others in the achievement of their ends. Self-interest is, of course, exhibited in the avoidance of the worst privations of coercive means, which can take a great variety of forms.

So, for example, it is quite consistent with their form of reasoning, and illustrates also what I called the more subtle structural means, that convinced Marxists should maintain that working for wages is a means of coercion in a capitalist society. The rationale of the assertion briefly, is as follows. Production in a capitalist society is not freely undertaken by producers and for the satisfaction of specific needs but in order that a certain small category of persons gain profits by the production of commodities for sale in a market. Once the means of production, which in this kind of society are complex and costly machinery and plant, become monopolised by a distinct group, all that is left to the remaining individuals is their skills or labour power. Because of the monopolisation of these means this latter group are forced into the position where the only way of obtaining their livelihood is to make their toil available to owners. This the owners obtain through the payment of wages, a system which frees them of a great number of traditional obligations which are typical for example of a feudal society, and even of the concern and care that a sensible slave-owner might be expected to exercise in the maintenance of his slaves. Given a free market in labour, worn out or inefficient wage-labourers are replaceable.[4]

This is a reasonable interpretation of the structure of productive relationships in early capitalist *laissez-faire* society though very contentious, particularly in the brief and simplified form given above, as a characterisation of Western industrial society today. Nonetheless it sufficiently well illustrates my point about 'structural' coercive means, which can be quite opaque to those persons who are involved in them. For, in the circumstances where the individual has known nothing but the system of wage-labour, the requirement to work for wages for some other person does not appear to him as a deprivation or an imposition. Indeed, the individual in a society in which the supply of labour exceeds the demand will, quite sensibly, regard himself as 'among the lucky ones' in having a job. He may even come to regard his employer with gratitude for having 'given' him work in such a society and accord him respect as a good, honest or fair man, on some relative basis. He may recognise that his own employer compares well in regard to conditions of employment, the wages he pays, the general concern he shows for his workpeople, and other characteristics of this kind, when compared with other employers. This appreciation on relative grounds of the difference between persons is in significant measure independent of a general understanding of the situation. The committed Marxist can as readily recognise, and where he is involved even appreciate, the relative differences between employers as individuals. This is unlikely, however, significantly to affect his judgment of capitalism, for it is the systematic structure of the relationships that he opposes rather than the individuals. Even where he regards employers as a class as selfish and rapacious he can temper the judgment with appreciation of the fact that the employer too is in a certain sense the dupe of the system. Certainly, the employer is deceived by appearances, indeed he plays some part in creating and promoting the structure of ideas which justifies the system and even deceives him. Such a structure of ideas, is called 'ideology'. We have met this notion before in connection with the tricky distinction between social structure and culture.

It is important to stress at this point that ideology is something distinctly more powerful than a set of 'excuses', or simple justifications. It is built into a substantial part of the society in which it develops. This will be evident from the remark that the class who benefit are themselves, in a perfectly comprehensible way, 'deceived' by ideology. It is a standard, orthodox way of understanding and explaining certain of the more important of social relationships and institutions in a society, as much as a mere excuse or apology for them. This also indicates something of a difficulty with the idea and the difficulty, that Weber grapples with in the notion of 'legitimation'. Like the answer given in terms of ideology, there is the recognition in Weber's answer to the question of why people obey, that for the most part societies are not normally based on *overt* coercion (one needs the qualification 'overt' in order to meet the point that, as we have just seen, it may be possible to interpret some relationships as coercive which are not normally regarded as such in the society in question).

In various societies, it appears, various modes of behaviour, including the acceptance of the 'right' of one person to give orders to others in the likely anticipation that they will be obeyed, are accepted as 'right and proper'. The three major types of legitimation that Weber proposes are: traditional, charismatic and rational-legal. The essence of them is that in a society characterised by a traditional form of legitimation the reply to the question 'Why should I obey you?' is 'Because this is the way things have always been done in the past'. The reply of the charismatically legitimated authority is 'Because *I* say so'. This is so terse as to need a little explanation.

The foundation of charismatic leadership is belief in the

extraordinary qualities or abilities of the individual. Consequently a reply to the question is barely possible for once the exceptional qualities of the individual charismatic leader are challenged the very basis of charismatic authority is undermined. This is the authority of the great revolutionary figures who defy established systems of authority. It is also a system of legitimation that has constantly to be renewed by means of successes and signs that the exceptional powers of the individual have not waned. Popular examples of charismatic leaders, usefully a very disparate group to put together (which underlines the fact that the charismatic leader is not necessarily 'good') range from Jesus Christ and certain other of the saints, through Mahatma Gandhi and John Kennedy to Adolf Hitler and Benito Mussolini. It is a useful reminder that not only saints but effective demagogues fall under this heading. Charismatic leadership, given the constant demand for signs of its continuance of the exceptional abilities is fundamentally unstable. It can be institutionalised or routinised; the papacy for example, one of the longest continuing institutions of authority, can be regarded as an institutionalisation of the original charismatic power vested by Jesus Christ in the apostle Peter and passed on to each successive Pope. Clearly, however, routinised charisma comes in such circumstances as these to be hardly distinguishable from traditional authority. The idea of charismatic leadership is rather more central to the understanding of revolutionary movements than of stable social structures, though as we shall see, since Weber employs what he calls 'ideal—type' concepts, even the charismatic form of legitimation remains of some interest in the explanation of the acceptance of authority structures.

Much the most central form of legitimation for our purposes, however is the form that characterises the complex modern societies with which we are centrally concerned. The reply to our question when this form of authority is challenged is something like 'I give orders in accordance with the authority vested in me by the law, or the rule book. The justification of the structure that gives me authority is in its rationality; it efficiently serves the function that it has been set up to achieve.' This is the most important one, because it is recognisably the standard justification. So much so, indeed, that it is reasonable to regard this as the only acceptable justification for authority. The other two forms of legitimation serve a useful purpose, perhaps, in reminding us that the rational-legal mode of justification of authority is not the only *possible* one.

There is an absolutely central distinction, we need to notice, between the concept of ideology, which we have exemplified in terms of the Marxist analysis of industrial society, where it plays such a central part in the reasoning, and the notion of legitimacy. That difference consists (rightly or not, for this is a complicated debate within sociology) in the attempted achievement of 'value-freedom' in the use of the Weberian notion. The recognition and revelation of both ideology and legitimation require the ability to stand back from the particular social reality in some measure. As we saw above, it was a significant help to have a reminder that authority has not always been and, indeed, is not in certain circumstances within our own kind of society, regarded as justified only in terms of effectiveness in the achievement of certain ends. To recognise this as an ideology one needs an alternative conception of what society could (or should) be like. The Marxist analysis provides this. *But*, if analysis of a situation is to be true to the fashion in which the persons themselves see it rather than the fashion in which it is seen by persons who have achieved some kind of 'enlightenment' on the way things 'really are', this is not acceptable. The implication that those who recognise ideology are better informed than those who accept certain reasonings as valid justification for the form of relationship must be abandoned. Any system of human organisation and relationship, it is argued, would have some set of justifications; a socialist society quite as much as a capitalist one would require an 'ideology'. The Marxist, it must in fairness, be said, is not without a reply to this, but we cannot pursue this complex debate further here. The point centrally at issue is that the notion of 'ideology' cannot fail to be evaluative and for the most part this is not denied in its use. Ideology is a 'cover' for some arrangement whether or not those who benefit from it recognise it to be so. Whether or not Weber achieves freedom from implications of this kind in respect of the notion of legitimation is perhaps less important than that there is an attempt to use it in a value free way that distinguishes it from ideology. *At any given time*, the account that is given of why people accept orders is to be regarded as the best account available even if, with hindsight, we come to regard their account as misconceived. It tells us about an element of the society's culture. It is only by a choice *external* to the social situation that one is trying to account for and to analyse, that the judgments of those involved in the situation can be 'bettered', and consequently this goes beyond description and analysis. By these standards the Marxist may promote an alternative ideology, and may even be able to claim with some justification that his ideology promotes a system in which the exploitive nature of capitalist society may be overcome, but he does not thereby escape ideology himself.

Legitimations are typical explanations, as given by the persons involved in the social situations, of why they accept the system of authority relationships that they do. This translates into the acceptance of the orders of certain persons because of a traditionally established position, because of the supposed exceptional abilities of the individual, or because of a particular set of competences operated within a circumscribed system. This last, associated with rational-legal legitimation, paraphrased in the way it is here, points up the relationship to another of Weber's key concepts, that of bureaucracy, as the major form of legitimation of key concern to us. But a passing remark above established the point that the forms of legitimation in Weber were to be re-garded as 'ideal—types', and a few words are required on this.

Traditional, charismatic and rational-legal legitimation are not in practice strictly separated from one another. The forms of legitimate order can merge. We have already had an example of how an essentially charismatic relationship can translate itself into a traditional form in the case of the papacy. Looked at from a different angle, that of our position as wouldbe analysts of the situation rather than observers of the social reality 'as it truly is', this is to provide for a flexible use of instruments that will allow us to detect subtly interwoven shades of relationship. Indeed the subtlety of analysis that these three forms of legitimation allow us alone, without recognition of the ideal-typical nature of the ideas, may sometimes make us wish that we had a less luxurious set of ideas available, for analysis can become extremely complex. However this may be, the way in which we may come to recognise both the ways of justifying social structures and also the *real* relationships that represent these ways of thinking is clear enough.

It is a commonplace enough matter to recognise that tradi-tional modes of justification may remain. 'Custom and practice' as the justification of many industrial practices is both the reason given for their continuance *and* an explana-tion of the fashion in which the particular jobs are done. From certain points of view such practices may not be the most rational or efficient. Similarly, in the same context the continuing influence of a shop steward may be attributed to charismatic qualities, to extraordinary competence in managing industrial disputes, or in the persuasiveness of his negotiating techniques. In this last case we will want to look for something more than mere skill or competence: what is required is the belief that no one else could be expected to do the job as well, that it is not a matter of rule-of-thumb competences which might be learned by others, but that individual qualities are involved.

The first of these examples may have suggested that in an analysis of real-life situations we should recognise that there are possible historical hangovers to be taken into account. Up to a point this is a justified inference, but we need to go further. To think of them as hangovers is to take a position on what the 'proper' forms of legitimation are and to favour something like the rational-legal justification. This is simply to be children of our time, if Weber was right in maintaining that this form of legitimation and its organisational expression, bureaucracy, has come to dominate twentieth-century industrial societies. It will not matter seriously in the analysis if we do not at the same time regard these kinds of structure and justification as simply 'irrelevant', irresponsible' or 'foolish', or with some similar value coloration.

The point about the types is that in any but the simplest situations we must anticipate finding them richly mixed up, and this in spite of the dominance in our time of rational-legal legitimation. Any ideal—type, as Weber himself strongly stressed, is a one-sided accentuation of certain features that one can recognise in real-life situations and both the form of legitimation and bureaucracy as its institutional extension are distinctly a dominant characteristic of our own time.[5]

Bureaucracy, rationality and social control

For our purposes it is not necessary to specify in full Weber's notion of bureaucracy, but something needs to be said about it, and about the idea to which it is closely related, that of rationality. This is another enormously complicated and ramified idea, but we will pursue its understanding only to the degree needed for our present concerns.

'Rationality' entails the notion of reasonableness, but also a good deal more. In its association with bureaucratic forms of organisation, rationality also entails the idea of efficiency, of the selection of means appropriate to ends. 'Rationality' of a kind, as we shall see, dominates the large-scale organisations that are such a striking feature of modern industrial societies. This form of rationality, as is indicated in Weber's linking of the terms in the notion of the rational-legal, is distinctly associated with rules, even though the rules need not be legal ones in a strict or even a usual sense. The rules, rather, are a clear specification of the appropriate way of behaving, or a clear limitation on what is *not* permissible. The term applies to both technical rules and to rules of interpersonal conduct, such as those governing the relationship between, for example, foremen and their subordinates.

Large-scale organisation necessitates close coordination of activities. This in its turn demands a great variety of performances that can be taken for granted. Varieties of skill are anticipated and performances are set down in such a fashion as to slot into one another and so achieve the wanted effect. This is the fashion in which much industry is recognisably conducted. It is clearly an ideal—typification, for absolute efficiency of this kind cannot sensibly be anticipated, so that there have to be back-up arrangements, contingency plans, standby operations and the like. The production line in the car factory is a common example. But it is not simply an industrial model, it conforms closely to a great deal of governmental and commercial organisation.

Looked at in this way, organisation takes on a distinctly mechanical (in the sense of mindless) and inhuman appearance. Why, if it is truly like this, is it tolerable to the people in it, or to the people in the society at large, even if they are not immediately involved? 'Legitimation' provides the answer to this in the case of the society at large; 'efficiency' has come to be the broadly accepted basis on which enterprises of all kinds are to be judged. And efficiency comes to mean economic efficiency, efficiency which is validated by accounting devices, themselves part of the bureaucratic machinery in operation. Broadly, operation of this kind is looked on as sensible and is believed to have a 'pay-off' in terms of the volume of goods and services delivered to society at large. This is plausible. It is also self-justificatory because it inhibits the setting up of the kind of new forms of relationship that might prove it to be less efficient than it appears.

Weber was obsessively concerned with this efficiency of bureaucracy, particularly governmental bureaucracy, because he believed it would crush out the whole range of individual human potentialities. This is more evident in accounting for the acceptance of the persons who are involved in the bureaucratic machinery. They are, of course, influenced also by the general commitment to the idea of efficiency as the achievement of large-scale bureaucratic structures, but bureaucratic organisation offers additional advantages. Among the more important of these is security. Perhaps with the governmental civil service organisations especially in mind Weber pointed to the fact of a career in the organisation, with an expectation of regular pay increments and progress up some of the rungs of a promotion ladder followed at the end of one's service with a pension, as being characteristic. Given normally efficient performance the individual need not fear dismissal. Bureaucracy offers security in a variety of ways, not least by providing a clearly specified set of roles for those operating within it, so that they 'know their place'—to whom they are responsible, who is responsible to them, and what their function is. In addition, devices to prevent the arbitrary exercise of power are instituted, so that on disciplinary matters, for example, there is likely to be a clearly codified procedure for dealing with complaints against an individual, arrangements for appeal to higher authorities and so on.

Once again it must be stressed that this is an ideal-type. This illustration indeed helps to clarify the nature of Weber's ideal-type formal actions. The typical organisation sketched out in these remarks may never be discovered in the perfection of all the characteristics that have been outlined; nonetheless it is a recognisable pattern. This type, furthermore is not simply plausible but also offers answers to such questions as 'Why do those involved in, and those subject to these arrangements accept them?' They answer a question, that is, of legitimation.

One point, absolutely central to our own concerns is only *implicit* in what has been said. Most notably, while the bureaucratic form of organisation can call forth a minimal kind of allegiance by satisfying people that they are getting a fair deal by working within its rules, it is incompatible with anything emotionally stronger. Strong *commitment* to such organisation is unusual: militant commitment, virtually a contradiction in terms. Structures of this kind have no use for such involvement. Cool logic and efficient performance of duties is what they call for; they cannot accommodate emotionality.

Once indicated this is clearly so. Bureaucratic organisation is distinguished by Weber from the forms of organisation where placement within the organisation is influenced by such things as kinship and friendship ties. Within the organisation itself friendship patterns that do arise are kept apart from the operation of the organisation itself; such allegiances are regarded as extraneous to the purposes of the organisation, and things to be guarded against. Equally in the relationships to persons outside the organisation the rule is equality of treatment except in so far as the persons dealt with are categorised in a variety of ways which make for discrimination between groups in the technical interest of the organisation itself. A large-scale manufacturing organisation is likely to discriminate, for example, between categories of bulk-buyers of their products and 'small' customers, but not on personalised grounds.

Many of these characteristics of large-scale organisations seems distinctly commonplace. But this fact reveals the broad acceptance of certain patterns of organisation and behaviour in our kind of society, to the point indeed that we have value-loaded terms for certain practices that go against the kind of code that has been exhibited, terms like nepotism, corruption, favouritism and the like.[6]

The two absolutely key concepts in our discussion of social control we now see to be solidarity and legitimation. The first of these is essentially characterised by its affective nature, while the second calls for justification which in our times is most commonly, though not exclusively, given in terms of rationality and efficiency. Sometimes we find solidary structures fiercely conflicting with legitimated ones, sometimes the legitimated structures apparently serve the solidary ones. There are even occasions when solidary structures appear to have become secondary to the legitimated ones.

In the next chapter we make use of industrial case studies to illustrate this major theme and some of the subsidiary themes that have emerged from our discussion.

An illustration:
social control in industry

4

Because there is much illumination to be had from considering the achievement and maintenance of social control in
terms of solidarity and legitimacy, it should not be assumed
that social control situations necessarily fall neatly into two
exclusive divisions. On the contrary, even the most evidently
solidaristic social grouping will be legitimated, while even the
most formalistic legitimated social relationship is likely to
have some element of solidarity.

Furthermore, it is difficult to envisage a situation in which,
to remind ourselves of Weber's definition of social action, our
actions can be regarded as 'oriented' to only one other person
or group. Consequently one should expect that in any but
the simplest situations there will be conflicts and tensions.
Not only between our commitments to different groups, but
also at different levels of legitimated activity, it is reasonable
to anticipate that decisions will from time to time be forced
upon us. We will have to choose between equally legitimate
demands or find some compromise between them. Together,
differences of solidary commitment and conflicting
legitimate demands make for a very complex set of possibilities.

Gouldner, in his book *Wildcat Strike*,[1] certain findings of
which we shall consider below, speaks of the 'saliences'
among various groups, by which he means the established sets
of broad preferences and commitments, the broadly taken-
for-granted attitudes and expectations. Such 'saliences'
provide for the rough categorising of situations and allow for

9

reasonably rapid response to situations in which tensions like those suggested may arise. Gouldner's book deals with an industrial situation, and this is the kind of situation in which the demands of legitimacy and solidarity may present themselves very sharply. In much of industry too (though not all, for some technologies prevent formation of them) small group relationships, which we have especially associated with solidarity and remote rule-governed relations, legitimated relationships—coexist.

It would not be accurate to regard the factory as the microcosm of the larger society, and it serves our purposes better because it is not. So, in the wider society we need hardly be aware of authority and the legal system. The principal source of contact for most of us is of an irritant kind, associated with parking and traffic misdemeanours. Within a factory, however, the authority system and a great variety of rules are inescapable, evident and ever present at all levels. The first legitimations of this activity, and of the relationships in industry are, for all that, much more general, societal legitimations, and in using industry as a case study to illustrate and develop the many themes that we have now considered we must turn first to the most general legitimations for working at all, and then to the legitimation of the actual *forms* that industrial organisations take.

'Why work?' seems an odd question. The very oddness, is an indication of how deeply entrenched certain attitudes are in our society. But these attitudes are not simply 'natural', as we can see by turning once again to Max Weber, this time to his book *The Protestant Ethic and the Spirit of Capitalism*.[2] If the question seems impossibly odd, simply recall that the notion of 'gentry' was applied to persons who did not need to work *and were not expected to*. Such work as they undertook might be regarded rather as a kind of genial eccentricity. In these circumstances it was *not* working that conferred status. All work other than that undertaken in certain 'professional' capacities (often distinguished in the early professions by being essentially voluntary, i.e., 'amateur'), was the prerogative of 'lower orders'.

The work ethic and the justification of authority in industry

Weber's book is concerned with explaining why industrial capitalism as we know it developed in the West and not elsewhere, where many of the necessary conditions of its development were also present. In brief, his conclusion is that only in western Europe did a set of attitudes and beliefs creative of a distinct psychological tension which provided the impetus for capital accumulation arise. These attitudes were associated with the Protestant Reformation. Our question 'Why work?' came to be answered in terms of the commitment that work was undertaken 'to the greater glory of God'. Behind that justification for work lay the strong psychological tension to seek for signs of God's grace and of 'election to His Kingdom', and worldly success was taken to be a sign of such election. Much of the plausibility of Weber's account of the beginnings of capitalism relies on this latter implication of the doctrine of predestination—the doctrine, that is that God had already determined who was to go to Heaven. Success in life was taken to be as good an indication as one could possibly have that God's favour had been bestowed, and this would be true of all believers, whatever their 'station in life'.

'Work is for the greater glory of God' is to be understood, in our terms, as an expression of a legitimation for work, something that both justifies it and gives an account of why it is desirable. There were secondary legitimations too, that 'honest toil' was a way of warding off temptation, for example. This indeed provides us with an example of the most *general* kind of legitimation. Such beliefs are, of course, not commonplace now, or if such legitimations still exist they find expression, for the most part, in a more secular form. Nonetheless, it can be argued that the 'Protestant ethic' is still with us, both as institution and as ideology. It is still broadly the case that work is regarded as something that everyone who is able to should engage in. Hence the seeming oddity of the question: justification is needed for not working, work is the legitimate activity *par excellence*. Legitimated activity need not find clear articulation though, as we saw, a characteristic of rational-legal legitimation is that an expression of the rationale for the activity will be available *if* called for. To the extent that a practice is taken for granted and never pondered as problematic its legitimation may be becoming traditionalised. Modern industrial societies are not exempt from that possibility. This will be the point reached when we respond that this is the way it always has been—how could it be otherwise?

The religious legitimation of work is now foreign to most of us, the activity rather has become institutionalised. This is not to say that the desirability that able persons should work is less strongly maintained. On the contrary, it is now more exclusively maintained than ever, even royalty now being justified in terms of its 'job', the social function that it performs, rather than in terms of its hereditary rights and privileges, as in the past.

The new expression of the rationale of work is implicit in these last remarks, the most common and central justification being in these essentially 'socialist' terms, that all should engage in work as a contribution to the society and to the wellbeing of fellow citizens. It would be wrong to regard this kind of rationale as discontinuous with the older religious legitimation, for it can readily be regarded not as essentially different from the old rationale but as a kind of secular version of it, the 'religious' commitment now being to the society rather than to God.

The institutionalisation of work exists in a great multiplicity of forms. Perhaps the most evident are the negative ones, so evident indeed as to make us wonder once again how they could ever be questioned. So, in spite of a commitment to welfare, very complicated administrative arrangements have been called into existence in the attempt to ensure that persons are not better-off (as the families of low-wage earners might well be) by being out of work than they would be in employment. Permission not to work is something to be achieved 'under licence', so to speak, a 'licence' such as the doctor's certificate of incapacity. The work attitude is built into the institutional structure of the society and into our own personalities as well. Not working is something that we have a bad conscience about, or failing that, something that we feel that we *ought* to have a bad conscience about. In this fashion it can be seen as a legacy of the 'Protestant ethic'.

It cannot be stressed too strongly that legitimation occurs at a great number of different levels. At different levels we may find that distinct paradoxes are created, for the seemingly appropriate response to a strongly legitimated activity may be in conflict or tension with another. We saw an example of this in the last paragraph, for we can recognise a legitimate requirement to the maintenance and support of one's family (a requirement underpinned in most cases by solidary commitment as well) as possibly being in conflict with the undertaking of an 'honest' job. However this may be, the work ethic is among the most general of social demands, and we have seen how it is most generally legitimated. It does not follow that the individual may not express his own commitment to work in other ways; all that follows is that for the most part there will be no inconsistency in practice between the individual's formulation and the more general one. There is no inconsistency, for example, between the social legitimation of work and the individual assertion that one works 'merely' to gain one's livelihood, or that one works to give one's family a reasonable standard of life.

But all legitimations need not fit neatly together, and not all obligations are universal, as the obligation to work is legitimated to be. Much more fragile are the legitimations as to whom one works for, under what conditions the work is undertaken, what is the extent of various persons' authority, and so on. We remain at a very general level in considering the legitimation of the 'right' to give orders in industry, but nonetheless move down one level from the work ethic in doing so, and find ourselves in rather less consensual realms.

Reinhard Bendix, in *Work and Authority in Industry*,[3] tackles such questions, treating them historically and cross-culturally. His concern is not with legitimation as such but with managerial ideologies. Clearly though, these are very closely related indeed. The variation in concern, as we have seen, centres on the degree of acceptance of the ideology, for an accepted ideology is, by definition, a legitimation for certain activities or for certain authority relationships, or more often than not, for both. Tyranny, for example, is *not* something that can be legitimated; it may be tolerated up to a point but beyond that point is maintained by the exercise of power. Legitimate domination can be provided with broadly accepted justifications, though these may change over time.

At the level of the actual workplace or enterprise, as we have already seen, the most general legitimation is the assertion of efficiency, the contention that everyone is fitted to his role in the organisational structure, that certain prerogatives must be maintained if the system is to continue to operate satisfactorily.

This, as can be seen from Bendix's book and other sources, is a fairly recent source of legitimation and by no means a totally stabilised one. It is contested from a number of positions. Among these are the older claims to legitimate control, grounded notably in the claims of property rights and investment risks. At its simplest the right to control in this case is simply grounded in the assertion that ownership confers such rights, that the owner or investor 'creates' the employment and does so at a risk to his own standard of life. This is often associated with a paternalistic gloss, especially in old-established firms; allegiance is called for because of the

74

established traditional concern of the firm for its employees' welfare. Alternatively, bureaucratic efficiency is attacked as being fraudulent. This is a particular response of academics and more radical activist workers, who may be promoting some alternative form of industrial organisation, such as workers' control. 'Efficiency' is seen by them as a claim that serves the interests either of managements or of owners who operate through them and use them as their instruments. In our time even the most general legitimations are in competition and subject to challenge, probably to a degree that was inconceivable in earlier historical periods.

An attack on the efficiency of a *particular* firm, however, may not constitute an attack on either the form of organisation or its legitimation, as we shall see. It is distinctly problematic for the interpreter of industrial action of various kinds whether the grounds of the action are the system of relations, certain personal antagonisms, some specific grievances, a diffuse discontent, or a blend of all these. In turning to some studies of industrial strife we shall consider the relationship of these in the context of the shifting and emerging forms of social control in the industrial enterprise. Before this we must discuss an illustration of the other side of our equation, 'solidarity'. A striking illustration, for it shows how readily certain legitimations of authority, with supposed implications well beyond that of mere commitment to a form of organisation, could be taken for granted to the point that solidary relationships appear as inexplicable.

The Hawthorne experiments

This is the name by which a very famous series of experiments, at first basically concerned with the discovery of the optimum conditions for productivity in industry, have become known. 'Hawthorne' is the name of the Chicago works of the Western Electric Company, where the experiments were conducted.[4] The briefest of accounts of the experiments, and the various interpretations of the findings will be enough for our purposes.

The earliest of these experiments was conducted by the Hawthorne management, without the support of Harvard University's Department of Industrial Research under Professor Elton Mayo, with whom the later work and its findings came to be especially associated. These were experiments with different levels of lighting intensity which invited further investigation because of the seeming oddity of the research findings. Increasing the illumination, they found, increased the output but returning to the original illumination level did not bring about a reduction of productivity to what it was before the experiment. Careful re-tests indicated, indeed, that as long as *some* experimental activity appeared to be going on, even when it involved making the physical conditions of work *less* satisfactory, something better than anticipated production would be achieved. Clearly there was some kind of 'interference effect' which the experiment introduced into the situation, an effect which has come to be known as 'Hawthorne effect'. These unanticipated experimental results prompted a series of further experiments, the Relay Test Room and Bank Wiring Room experiments, which became progressively more concerned with social relationships and less and less with physical conditions of work. The outcome was the discovery of the 'informal group' in industry, effectively, the discovery that within an industrial enterprise a complex of 'natural' systems of social relationships develop which are in significant measure out of control of the official system of authority and organisation.

It came as a surprise to the experimenters and their sponsors at this time that workpeople are not essentially isolated atoms, that they do 'combine', that they develop their own conceptions of what is a fair day's work, of what their proper relationship should be to one another and to supervisors and officials. They had, that is to say, their own norms and values, their own conceptions of a status hierarchy and their own conceptions of legitimacy; but in our terms rather than that of the experimenters, they had discovered solidarity relationships within the factory.

This may seem a distinctly unsurprising set of findings in the context of our own times and is indeed not to be properly understood and appreciated, much less made the basis for the observations that are to come, without an understanding of the social background of the experiments. This will be necessary too to an understanding of the response of the experimenters to the findings, for these become an interesting part of the data for us. Part of the explanation of the feeling of real 'discovery' in this for the experimenters, for the management, and indeed for other social scientists and interested lay persons of the time is implicit in the earlier remark about workpeople as essentially 'isolated atoms'. Even now there may be reason to question the inevitable existence of informal groups in industry.

They should not be confused with the trade union organisation in industry. Trade unions played no part in the Hawthorne experiments for the simple reason that they did not exist in the plant studied, where there was merely a so-called 'factory union'. (These are organisations which are not independent of management and consequently cannot be autonomous representative organisations of workers' interests.) For our purposes it is well to distinguish strongly between the union as an official, structured form of organisation—and these established informal relations between workpeople.

'Isolated atoms' was the general conception of workpeople in industry and the customary premise when considering various aspects of management policy in regard to workpeople. This is consistent with the legalistic idea, of course, of the relationship between employer and employee as being an individual contract formally entered into between free and equal partners. It is also consistent with an earlier and much favoured conception of efficient management practice which the Hawthorne experiments did much to challenge, and which is associated with the name of F. W. Taylor and the 'Scientific management'[5] movement. Taylor promoted the doctrine of 'one best way' of undertaking every industrial task, and a 'functional' conception of industry which regarded it as a place where both worker and management were striving for the best possible financial return for the least physical effort. Any relationship which stood in the way of this achievement was, by his standards, irrational and unwarranted. Thus, even though he seems to have been not unaware of solidary relationships between individuals, he regarded such relationships as worthy only of condemnation. He was certainly not provoked to study them, for as he saw it such relationships simply stood in the way of what, if they only knew better, workpeople themselves would have seen was their own best interests.

This movement is strongly associated with work study and time-and-motion studies in industry and has had an enormous influence on managerial practice. In part, of course, we can understand this in terms of the distinct material advantages that it offered to management; but it has a rather more subtle 'spin-off' in a form of managerial legitimation, for this scheme presents the manager as the competent 'functional' official, a man whose position is justified by the 'scientific management' skills through which he serves everyone who is associated with the company, a competence calling for high levels of knowledge and intelligence. Notably, this is a legitimation that goes beyond simple ownership claims and paves the way for an ideology of professional management.

While Taylor's picture was of workpeople as isolated 'economic' men, men whose sole aim was to achieve a maximum reward for a minimum effort, the Hawthorne investigations revealed 'social' man, an individual who established a complex set of norm-governed relationships, for whom the level of income was a consideration but was not the exclusive concern of the individual. This new attitude to the motivation of workpeople created a new and alternative school of thought, and the development of new kinds of 'personnel management' techniques. It came to be known as the 'Human relations' movement.

From our viewpoint we see both the 'discovery', that is the recognition of the existence of informal relationships in industry, and a change in the legitimation of work, in a rather different fashion than did the experimenters and supporters of the new industrial relations doctrines. Of this first point, it is hard for us now to put ourselves in the position of these industrial managers and researchers, but clearly we can see the 'revelation' of the informal work group as much less a 'discovery' than the development of a willingness to see what had long been there to see, but which it served certain interests not to notice.

Notably, the effect of the discovery of the informal work group, while introducing many very significant changes in industrial relations practices, carefully maintained the established authority relationships in industry, and this at a time when trade union and political pressures were subjecting them to a challenge. It has been a justified criticism of the uses to which the Hawthorne experiments findings were put that they were quite distinctly managerially biased. In spite of the strongly antagonistic debates between supporters of 'Scientific management' and of 'Human relations', there is little to choose between the positions with regard to the interpretation of workers' activities. These activities are not effectively regarded as more rational by Human relations exponents. Consequently what evolved as a practical response to the discovery of the informal group was a variety of techniques, constituting a mixture of therapy for workers— sessions in which they can get their problems and grievances off their chests—and a range of devices for controlling and accommodating the informal group. This is consistent with the original concerns of the research, which were with the constraints on productivity.

It was not part of the Hawthorne researchers' interpretation of their findings then, to regard the formal and informal
relationships within the factory as equal in status and significance. They continued to regard the workplace as a 'unitary'[6]
phenomenon, an organisation which served the best interests
of everyone engaged in it, in which both the determination of
aims and their achievement were the province of management
and their expert advisers, and with the techniques of production and the like, including 'man management', being essentially technical in nature. The alternative, that an industrial
organisation is essentially a rather unstable association of
very diverse interests and concerns in which 'accommodations' achieved through a bargaining process are the fundamental, if often quite temporary, solution to the problem of
establishing an appropriate relationship between management
and workpeople (a pluralistic conception of the workplace)
did not occur to them.

We must not preen ourselves as being especially clever
compared with Taylor and Mayo. We are right in seeing that,
however unwittingly, they each presented different formulations of an historically more acceptable justification for the
form of organisation of industry. They both provided a legitimation for an established form of authority relationship,
buttressed by bodies of reasoning that offered a foundation
for supplementary specialist skills, such as that of the time-
and-motion study man, and the personnel management
specialist. But it is entirely consistent with the climate of
opinion of their times and their position in the larger social
structure as specialists concerned with industrial efficiency
that they should interpret their findings as they did. To
understand this is to realise the significance of legitimations
of various statuses and activities in other parts of the social
structure, and how powerful these cultural products can be.

A much criticised feature of both Human relations and
Scientific management modes of thought is that they failed
to see 'beyond the factory gate', that they regarded the factory

as a closed world of interest. This was perhaps rather more logically acceptable in Taylor's reasoning than in Mayo's, for the factory for Taylor was simply the place where men went to earn their livings. It was a distinct weakness of Human relations thought, however, to fail to realise that the norms and values, attitudes and allegiances of informal groups in industry might be very strongly related to external associations and concerns.

Solidary relationships, such as those evidenced in the informal groups discovered in the course of the Hawthorne experiments though 'natural' are not inevitable. Most evidently, as has been suggested, there are occasions when job technology prevents the significant formation of groups. Literal lack of association among workpeople in the same enterprise, the noise of machinery or spatial distance between them, may be enough to inhibit their significant development.

In some measure the working conditions may even be manipulated to prevent the establishment of such groups. But two other broad possibilities also present themselves. The first of these is the acceptance of the ideology of work as a simple means to an end, *coupled with* some sound reasons, evidence or simply strongly held belief that the formation of solidary relationships would undermine this simple singular purpose. The so-called 'affluent worker' of our own time has been proposed as an example of this. The second is the circumstance where no common interest, no pay-off from a solidary relationship, is anticipated. Such pay-off may not be straightforwardly economic, but may be in terms of security advantages, social satisfactions, even the sheer ability to get some measure of control over their working lives. For Michel Crozier, this last point, the need for some measure of autonomy, is of the essence of the relationships among workers employed in bureaucratic organisations.

We shall turn to this shortly but let us first turn to some work which was prompted by the

Hawthorne researches and their perceived shortcomings.

T. Lupton, in *On the Shop Floor*,[7] reports his findings from participant observation studies of two firms to which he gave the pseudonyms The Wye Garment Company and Jays Electrical Components. He too was concerned with the systems of control which operate in industry, but particularly directed his attention to the logic of workers' responses. These we have seen were characterised in the Hawthorne studies as irrational.

The principle interesting outcome of these two studies from our point of view was the different form which the solidary groupings took. In the one case they operated in such a way as to stabilise and support managerial legitimation and control. In the second, a complex mode of control was established through informal groupings which effectively compensated for irregularities of earnings and created a relationship with management in which, as Lupton puts it, 'different values about a fair day's work, and about "proper" work behaviour, could exist side by side'.[8]

In Jay's, however, where strong solidary groupings existed, social control devices in our most immediate and evident understanding of the notion were in evidence among the workpeople. Lupton was sensitive to the variety of techniques employed even before undertaking his investigation, and one of the most striking and delightful examples of the informal network of controls is provided from his earlier experience. He recounts how, as an apprentice engineer, he had become involved in a work task that had been set for him and had become oblivious to the passing of time until he heard the 'buzzer' which indicated official finishing time. But normal practice among the workers was to finish about fifteen minutes before this, and their response to this breach of established practice though simple and unextreme was tailored precisely to the needs of establishing and maintaining commitment to the men's own pattern of relationships and behaviour. Lupton puts it thus:

[When] I looked up I found myself surrounded by a group of men who had obviously been watching me for some time. . . . Nothing was said, but their looks made it clear that I would soon become unpopular if I persisted in observing official times. . . . In time I learned other lessons about the customs and usages of the shop. To work too quickly was to be labelled a 'teararse' and to be at least partly shut out from the friendly give and take of the shop and from the spontaneously formed 'scrounging groups' which . . . assembled in secluded corners of the shop for unofficial tea-breaks and discussions.[9]

A judicious mixture of threat of punishment and reward set in a context of learning as to what the workshop situation is 'all about' and where allegiances lie.

The discovery of this kind of structure of relationship that from a managerial point of view constitutes a kind of 'under-world' in industry, and the variety of devices of control constitute a significant part of both the Hawthorne investigations and of Lupton's case studies. Lupton speaks of 'teararses' (those who tended to work too hard by the informal standards) and 'scroungers' (those who worked too little), just as the Hawthorne investigators had taken note of the conceptions of 'rate-buster' and 'chiseler' in the earlier investigations, and of the techniques that the workpeople had for bringing behaviour into line with their informal standards of what was a reasonable day's work.

In Jay's, however, to return to our main point concerning the basis of informal organisation, Lupton shows that it was far from being the case that rationality is a prerogative of managements while informal groups establish themselves simply to satisfy fundamentally emotional and companionable needs. He shows indeed, that the worker association satisfied distinctly rational ends. These consisted in a complex set of devices for stabilising income, the 'fiddle', as it was known to both management and workers alike.

There are many reasons why the workers in the other factory, the Wye Garments factory, did not respond in a similar way. We need not consider the details, for it is rather more important to us to indicate simply the extensive range of social control formations that can establish themselves and the different blend of legitimation and solidarity that they represent. Jay's provides an example of an informal structure that is so clearly formalised that 'informal' hardly seems the appropriate term to apply to it; it was a parallel structure to that provided by management and one which provided for an element of rationality the managerial system had been unable to accommodate. It is strongly legitimated in terms of service to that need but it is no less solidary a relationship, for it constitutes a commitment to the individuals who are part of it and the form of social relationships which it has developed to serve their needs. In this case, they supplement the formal structure and enhance it as a means of gaining a livelihood in an acceptable way. But in the Wye factory in Lupton's terms, the 'will to control' was absent. This is not to say that informal groups were not present, but that they expressed and served a set of rather different needs. The major solidary relationship, furthermore, extended beyond the workpeople themselves to many of the supervisory staff. Lupton notes that this was typical of the industry and remarks how in one firm some workers had even asked permission to strike in protest at the dismissal of a manager. Again, in his own words: 'The lack of "will to control" was also associated with the close identification of some workers with the management of the firm. . . . There was not a wide social gulf between workers and managers.'[10] The firms too tend to be of a paternalistic kind, and consequently bridge the gap, or smudge the distinction between clearly legitimated and clearly solidary social relationships. We shall have an illustration later of the dynamics of breakdown of a 'paternalistically legitimated' workplace in considering Lane and Roberts study of a 'Strike at Pilkingtons', but before doing this, let us consider an extreme case of a legitimated structure, and an equally extreme expression of the fashion in which solidary structures develop to combat the formal authority.

'The Bureaucratic Phenomenon'

This is the title of a recent powerful work by Michel Crozier[11] on the nature of bureaucratic organisation, again based on case studies. Crozier's critical target in this book is bureaucratic organisation itself. We have seen that Weber by no means approved of bureaucracy but regarded it as the most effective means of achieving the goals set for it. His point was that unsatisfactory as it might be in terms of the long-term undermining of individual initiative and emotional commitment, so that men become 'little cogs in great machines', it was difficult to envisage such organisation being superseded, simply because it 'worked'. It was the means of achieving ends, and perhaps the *only* means of achieving those ends that call for very complex coordination of skills, a demand that characterises our complex industrial civilisation. Crozier, however, contends that bureaucratic organisation is in fact intensely *inefficient*. It is so, in his view, because it cannot learn from its errors; bureaucratic organisation becomes involved in 'vicious circles'. These vicious circles stem from the natural response of individuals who seek autonomy, who need some measures of control over their day-to-day working lives and effectively find devices to obtain this measure of control. But the very rigidity of bureaucratic organisation, its extremely limited means of adaptation and accommodation to such needs, automatically ensures that the precisely wrong response will be made. For Crozier, and this is quite a reasonable reading of Weber on bureaucracy, a bureaucratic organisation inevitably responds to organisational breakdowns and perceived inefficiencies by tightening up the control of old rules or by introducing new ones. But since the need for some control over their affairs is by no means assuaged by this, all that this tightening up of the rules effectively results in is the discovery of ever new and more subtle means of evasion. The new techniques in their turn provoke further rules and control devices and so the vicious circles of rule-making and rule-avoidance take yet another turn.

Crozier's thesis is perhaps a little undermined for us in so far as he modestly limits his claims regarding the generality of his ideas to the French workers who were the subjects of his case study. Commenting specifically that English workers are perhaps rather more compliant, Crozier remarks that the drive for autonomy may be a distinct characteristic of French workers, derived from their culture. He also regards French bureaucracy as having significant features that distinguish it from those of other states. The monopoly industrial organisation is also rather specially selected to meet his need for a special extreme case to serve his investigation technique. We need not become too deeply embroiled in a discussion on this point, for our concern, with the nature of legitimation and solidarity and its forms and combinations is in any case of a rather more abstract kind. However, it is noticeable that the techniques and devices that these French workers employ are, in fact, distinctly like those which are documented in case studies of British industrial workers, some of which we have already looked at. There is the nice case, for example, of the missing schedules. A device by means of which maintenance men established some measure of autonomy, not only *vis-à-vis* management groups but we shall see also in connection with other groups, depended upon their monopolising certain functions. As Crozier put it:

> [Both] production workers and supervisors [are prevented] from dealing in any way with machine maintenance . . . the one unforgivable sin of a machine operator is to 'fool around' with her machine. Maintenance and repair problems must be kept secret itself as a rule-of-thumb skill. They completely disregard all blueprint and maintenance directions, *and have been able to make them disappear from the plants*. They believe in individual settings exclusively, and they are the only ones to know these settings. These and all the other tricks of the trade are learned through companionship on the job. Every job is done individually and there is a great deal of solidarity for learning purposes and whenever there is a difficult problem.[12]

The 'missing schedules' would be recognised by sociologists of industry as exemplifying a kind of technique exploited, according to the actual possibilities that present themselves in specific circumstances, quite commonly. It constitutes one possibility among a range of possibilities for the protection of a group of activities from the encroachment of 'bureaucracy' in the limited sense of 'reduction to rule' of the activities. It is distinctly *not* culturally specific.

Crozier has, we shall see, introduced a number of important new dimensions into our discussion of the solidarity element in social control, observations which help to give depth to the idea. Before exploring these further let us dispose of some possible impediments to our discussion. In particular we need not become too engaged in the apparent differences between Crozier and Weber. In part, these differences stem from differences of definition and of main concerns of the two scholars. The definitional problems are notorious. A recent study of the concept of bureaucracy lists no less than seven major *groups* of meaning that have been given to the term.[13] The outcome of these differences in definition is that it could be argued from Weber's viewpoint that 'bureaucratisation' had not effectively taken place at the levels with which Crozier is most concerned. The power of bureaucracy in part resides in its ability to provide stability and security, and Crozier is concerned with those groups—the workpeople, not the bureaucrats themselves even of a minor kind—to whom bureaucracy in that sense of the idea has not been effectively extended. Efficiency and rationality pose similar kinds of problem. In our terms it is rather more important to see that if Crozier is right concerning the disaffection shown by workpeople in the organisations which he studied what is indicated is that a balance of relationships that favours solidary formations rather than legitimated ones exists. But we shall see shortly that 'legitimated' structures of an unofficial kind may have developed. So strong, however, are the antagonisms that he portrays that it is reasonable to suggest that the legitimation to work in these organisations and to obey the instructions of those formally in charge probably derives much more significantly from the wider culture than it does from the organisation itself. The organisations may indeed have a negative contribution to make to wider social legitimations. There is some evidence for this in the persistent assertions of the 'inefficiency' of management. For, whatever 'efficiency' may be regarded as meaning to workers and whatever they regard as the indicators of it, the efficiency of the productive arrangements in the society is promoted as one of the strongest legitimations for that form of authority.

But Crozier also introduces a differentiation among groups of workers that we have not had cause to take notice of before, and thus introduces a new dimension of realism into our discussion. It will not do, we will realise on reflection, to regard all workers as comprising a single solidary group. This is not to deny this as a possibility but, as we shall see, special circumstances like those associated with strike action are likely to be the necessary basis. This is consistent with two things. First, our contention that solidary groupings, in our sense, are distinctly limited in scale. Second, that there is a very distinct breakdown of legitimacy that draws the groups together to form new social structures. *Par excellence*, the strike is the denial of legitimacy to those with formal authority.

It would be wrong to regard legitimated structures as being exclusive to formally authorised people, and this point is nicely brought out by Crozier in distinguishing between the various worker groups. From the point of view of the official organisation there is, indeed, what might be called a 'shadow' organisation of power. Certain groups of production workers, he shows, cannot choose anything but the most limited autonomy. Their choice is between compliance with management aims and directives or a kind of alliance with the maintenance workers. But this is not a solidary arrangement in our sense, except in so far as it develops into a system of mutual cooperation and trust between the individuals. It is a compromise arrangement that is selected among options—something persistently in tension, legitimated as the 'best possible option' and in part on broad conceptions of worker allegiances. Notice that this latter is not 'solidarity', it is reflective and rationalised and would be formulated and promoted as an articulate set of norms and values. In addition, the status and power divisions are an 'imposition' rather than a natural development. The nature of the tension too, will be clear, if one reflects that, however useful and effective the arrangement with the maintenance workers may be, whenever there is cause for sensitivity to their ability to manipulate relationships within the factory the production workers are likely to regard their 'authority' as usurped. It is a merely secondary legitimated authority if the official authority in the workplace remains less than crassly inefficient or not in breach of what is seen as proper managerial behaviour.

Crozier underlines this point and shows how it can operate as a social control mechanism which limits the extremes to which the maintenance men go *vis-à-vis* the production workers.

[It] is an important element of the [production workers' group] strategy to keep their alliance with the maintenance crew. At the same time this alliance must be viewed as a dangerous one. It must not go too far and lead to certain consequences. Maintenance people must be warned about possible limits. . . . Maintenance people sense the hostility around them. . . . Thus, this pressure is a very efficient sort of social control, and one may hypothesise that it keeps maintenance people well within the limits of what is culturally acceptable.[14]

The pattern of relationships in industry then, can be very complex. Legitimated structures, we have seen, are not exclusive to the official organisation, but can extend to power and authority structures which develop in an autonomous way.

Solidarities too, are complex and do not necessarily develop along lines which need appear most evident and 'natural' to the observer. They may serve a great variety of needs, from straightforward companionable needs which pose little or no challenge to the legitimated formal structure, to 'counter-organisations' which may challenge cultural standards of legitimate practice or even be regarded as supporting them in a somewhat eccentric way. Any reasonably unprejudiced observer of industry can recount informal practices engaged in by workpeople which improve efficiency, which 'oil the works', practices, indeed, which it can be seen have all too evidently been working when workers have some cause to be resentful and to withdraw their day-to-day 'cooperative' practices. And we must not forget that this all happens within an historical dimension; allegiances shift, subtle changes take place in the interpretation of what is 'proper' and 'fair'. Established arrangements in industry are constantly at risk from change of personnel, pressures of the market, technological development, and so on. So certain patterns of legitimation (secondary, of course, to such general cultural commitments as the 'work ethic' that we considered earlier, but nonetheless important in their place) are challenged. Gouldner throws some light on this, though we do not entirely share his analysis. He also introduces for the first time a discussion of the place of that very complex phenomenon in terms of our social control interests, the trade union.

'Wildcat Strike' and 'Patterns of Industrial Bureaucracy'

These are the titles of Gouldner's two classic studies,[15] the first of which we have had cause to comment on in passing. This is effectively a case study and analysis of the 'wildcat' strike (that is, 'unofficial' in the sense of not promoted by the union officials) which occurred at one of the factories belonging to an organisation to which Gouldner gave the pseudonym 'General Gypsum Company'. The second book is an attempt to draw more general conclusions from the study and to develop Weber's concept of 'bureaucracy' on the basis of the empirical findings. It is very close to our present concerns in discussing the patterns of legitimacy that had developed in the company.

The wildcat strike developed through a number of stages. It was clearly prompted in part by a number of external circumstances. In addition to a change in market pressures and the availability of younger and tough-minded potential new management a restructuring of the firm's management was in part prompted by the death of the old manager ('Doug'), around whom Gouldner reports a kind of legend as having established itself. 'Doug' thus came to be the symbol of a regime which the workpeople regarded as a better and happier time. The strike was associated with a wage claim, and Gouldner usefully notes what has perhaps become a near commonplace among industrial sociologists but is nonetheless distinctly relevant to our discussion, that the wage claim is effectively the universal justification for industrial action. As he puts it, '[The] wage issue involves claims about which workers feel most fully confident. In a sense a wage demand is always legitimate.'[16] It has since been many times remarked that a money argument can act as the catalyst of grievances which up to that point have not found what workers themselves can articulate and justify as a 'proper' cause of industrial dispute. We shall see this at work in the British setting at Pilkington's glass works which we consider next. But for Gouldner the wage demand was not the crux of the matter at the General Gypsum Company's factory. It was, rather, the collapse of what he calls the 'indulgency pattern', which was at the heart of the dispute.

The 'indulgency pattern', simply put, was an established give and take that had developed between the old management and the men. The men characterised this as 'leniency'. It expressed itself in such things as lack of close supervision, clemency in respect of lateness, the availability of some over-time to supplement income more or less at the request of workers. It extended to a rather unusual system of work allocation in which the individual worker had some measure of control as to the particular supervisor under which he would work. Even what might well be regarded as pilfering of raw materials and use of equipment was broadly tolerated. It was the tightening-up of control and the removal of indul-gencies such as these to which Gouldner assigns major responsibility for the strike.

In *Patterns of Industrial Bureaucracy*, Gouldner general-ised these findings to suggest that Weber's model of bureauc-racy was inadequate, that three models rather than one could be established. To these three models of bureaucracy he gave the titles: Mock, Representative, and Punishment-centred. The essence of the distinction between these resides in distin-guishing who effectively formulated the rules within the organisation and consequently how they are respected and maintained. In the first case, the rules are an imposition from outside the actual workplace; since they are not the expres-sion of values of either management or men they are not taken very seriously, and indeed are avoided if possible when other interests make it advantageous to do so. Representative bureaucracy is clearly associated with the 'old' system of management at the General Gypsum Company. It represents a kind of consensus solution of the problem of the formula-tion of rules, for both management and men initiate the rules and formulate them as their own. In such cases there is not normally a problem of how to deal with breach of rules. The major source of social control will be those two forms that have been rather overworked in the literature on social control, guilt and shame. The third form of bureaucratic organisation is characterised, as the name suggests, by the dominance in rule-making and the control over rule-observance by one party. Gouldner regards this as being a possibility for *either* management *or* workers. The domination of one party or the other is achieved by the infliction of punishments of various kinds. The punishments that workers might employ are presumably such things as withdrawal of cooperation.

Gouldner's three types of bureaucracy pose distinct problems. Their consideration is useful in prompting us to reflect once again on the nature of bureaucracy, and the closely associated question of the meaning of 'legitimation'. In our terminology a little reflection will convince one that what Gouldner has called 'representative bureaucracy' is perhaps better regarded as one of two possible arrangements. The first of these comes nearer to being, with a necessary caveat, a 'solidary' system. What has made this less than evident is the fact that we quite properly take any factory system to be an authority system. Much the most important and relatively unstressed factor about the pre-strike factory organisation, however, is the affinity of interests of managers and men. This has a clear connection with the fact that the Head Office of the firm was some distance away from the works and that all grades of employee at the factory had 'local' affiliations. A local community 'social control' system was operating to establish certain strong solidarities and some tensions between the 'legitimations' of the factory and of the local community. We see that a too rigid distinction has been drawn between management and men, with the consequence that 'solidarities' across this boundary have been ignored.

We have no special definitional rights over terms, but Gouldner's usage is in some respects misleading. There is for example, a strong asymmetry between the 'punishment', availability of workpeople and managements, which obscures the fact that in a certain very strong sense the organisation, in the final analysis, 'belongs' to the owners. The final sanction or 'punishment' is, indeed, to take the 'employment' away, in other words, close down or transfer the business. On similar grounds, representative bureaucracy is a rather utopian conception. It may be better regarded, in our way of looking at this, as a possible fashion of legitimating such a structure. But it would inevitably carry a measure of deception, for it effectively respresents a *choice* of management to present the arrangement in this way. It constitutes one of the most subtle forms of social control to convince a group that they are equal partners. The fact of this being an *option* of a management, however, shows the 'equality' to be that much one-sided. We have certain choices as to how to regard the set-up. In certain respects it may be as well to regard the factory set-up before reorganisation as hardly bureaucratised at all, as being an essentially 'traditional' structure. The truly bureaucratic structures were at the remote Head Office, and they did have the final powers we have noted. What we see here are new structures of legitimation being evolved, and it is clear that this does not simply mean 'happening'; it involves powers and pressures, the decline and even the 'putting to death' of old solidarity structures, for they 'die' if the appropriate environment ceases to exist which supported them. For all that there were later adjustments Gouldner makes it quite clear that the old system of relationships had no hope of being re-established.

In our way of reasoning, then, although we need some leeway in the term so that we can usefully speak of more and less bureaucratic structures, the saga of the General Gypsum Company is better understood as the (effective) attempt to *introduce* truly bureaucratic structure into an organisation, to introduce legitimated arrangements where solidary ones had previously operated.

The union played a curious part in the strike at General Gypsum. Gouldner documents how the strike was 'wildcat' rather than official, due to certain internal machinations and personal antagonisms. This can perhaps provide something of a corrective to the conception of the trade union as the paradigm representative of solidarity. But there is something missing in this account, looked at from a British perspective. It may be that this is a fair reflection of the difference in organisation and commitment of British and American trade unionism, but at General Gypsum the union appears as a remote kind of structure which seemingly overcorrects the image of solidarity. The result is that it appears to play a curiously negative and non-central part in Gouldner's account. We will find only a small measure of affinity in this respect—but rather more in others—between this case and the one which follows; this is also the case study of a strike, though twenty years and the Atlantic Ocean separate them.

'Strike at Pilkington's'

Lane and Roberts provide an account in this book of the industrial dispute which resulted in a 'wildcat' strike at Pilkington's Glass Works in St Helens, Lancashire, in April of 1970.[17] They capture the interest of the book for us, though it is a different interest from theirs, in their Introduction, where they write:

> Any strike amounts among other things to a crisis in an established system of authority. The Pilkington strike was a crisis not only for the firm but also for Britain's third largest union, for by the end of the stoppage the nucleus of a sizeable breakaway union had been created.

An 'established system of authority' is, of course, a legitimated structure and the breakdown of the old legitimation is clearly of central interest. But the study also provides a most unusual account of something much rarer even than an on-the-spot account of a strike which, rightly, Lane and Roberts note is very rare. That is, the attempt to set-up a breakaway union. We have noted that the union is, with justification, regarded as a type-case of a solidary organisation. There is some reason for this. At its best a trade union serves interests which are held by large numbers of workpeople as so self-evident as to be in no need of articulation. This is reinforced in the day-to-day association with other workers who evidently regard their union in the same fashion. It legitimates its authority in terms of these interests, creating the paradox that its legitimacy can be regarded as grounded in solidarity. But clearly, in the situation reported by Lane and Roberts the General and Municipal Workers Union had either never had this paradoxical form of legitimation (but something perhaps more nearly like the legitimation afforded to the management of a firm), or this legitimacy broke down in the situation that developed. The first of these options is, in fact, distinctly more plausible. The solidary response was expressed in the breakaway union that emerged, but especially among the members of the Rank-and-File Strike Committee, the leaders of the strike.

Here, then, we have an account of a very complex articulation of solidary commitments breaking down while others evolve and of old legitimations losing their force. Like the General Gypsum dispute the Pilkington strike was associated with a pay dispute and was triggered by a seemingly trifling incident concerning an error in payments, which management were certainly willing to rectify, but which escalated into a significant wage claim.

One of the clear bases of the claim to legitimacy of Pilkington's was grounded in its strong paternalistic traditions. Management regarded Pilkington's as a firm with concern for its employees, and it is clear that in significant measure this kind of regard was recognised and regarded as a worthy feature. This is different from, but worth comparing with the indulgency pattern of General Gypsum.

An interesting remark recorded by Lane and Roberts and their comment on it is a clue to the continuing belief in this kind of concern, challenged only by one of the most militant of the strike leaders:

> The [Rank and File Strike Committee Member] who said: 'The top management haven't got a bloody clue of what's going on. But I suppose if they did it wouldn't help. In fact I think they'd be a bloody sight tighter if they did know,' was *almost on his own* because there was the strong implication amongst all the rest—bar

the militants—that if top management *had* been in touch things would have been much better.[18]

This basis of legitimation was strongly held, though there was sensitivity to the old relationship perhaps being less firm than previously. Nonetheless, as the quotation above indicates, an intermediary—middle management—could be charged with having undermined the 'true' relationship between the owners and the men.

It is fascinating here to recall the most general legitimations of authority which we considered at the beginning of the chapter, for both workpeople and salaried management at the Pilkington Glass Works clearly still regarded ownership, albeit qualified as 'enlightened ownership', as an important basis for an authority relationship. What is clear, too, is that whatever the relationship had been in the past the plausibility of the paternalistic relationship as something more than an ideology—that is to say, as something having an evident basis in reality—was clearly declining. Lane and Roberts make it clear why this is so.

[The] vast increase in the scale of operations, particularly since the end of the Second World War, has meant that members of the family have just not been able to exercise the oversight over the running of the firm that once they could and have had to rely increasingly upon career managers who, no matter how much they might have imbibed the tradition of the company, will not have experienced the company as a *personal* thing in the way that family members have.[19]

The breakaway union (the attempt that is which the Rank-and-File Strike Committee made to form a 'new' union which would more effectively represent their interests, than the 'official' General and Municipal Workers Union) was a response in part to the belief that they had been 'let down' by the union. But Lane and Roberts also indicate a seemingly strange but convincing parallel between the firm and the union. That parallel consisted in what they regarded as the distinctly 'paternalistic' nature of the union, a large-scale, remote, bureaucratic organisation, which from a distance

Social control

claims both to be the servant of its members and to know what is best for them. 'Paternalism' here may seem to be a little stretched to cover both cases, but if we bear in mind that we are here concerned with the rough parallels that people draw rather than careful academic distinctions the collapse of the 'paternal' legitimation as a prop for both the trade union and the firm comes to seem rather more plausible. This emphasises the danger of following the common conception of trade unions as 'solidary' structures that we have remarked upon.

For indications of solidarity and its dynamics we have to turn especially to the militants of the Rank-and-File Strike Committee. Lane and Roberts convey well what an emotionally intense and personal kind of relationship is entered into by people who take on a leadership role of this kind. This is the kind of situation in which socialisation as a deep formative relationship is clearly at work. It is also, as the book strikingly illustrates, a distinctly dynamic process. At the end of the day these militants can say, 'This strike has been a bloody education'. For it is in these solidary relationships clearly that the old structures of legitimation truly dissolve as the new insights are forged and cognitive restructuring (the reinterpretation of social reality) at one or more levels occurs.

The strike here may be seen as associated with, though this is not to attribute cause which can be much more complicated, the weakening and breaking down of the old modes of legitimation. But this says very little about what new modes will be established, and with what intensity. It still remains important that the new grounds for a legitimate relationship be articulated and 'sold'. Those groups like the Rank-and-File Strike Committee who, forced to rethink, and supported in that rethinking for a while with the security and intensity of their solidary relationship with each other, may be rather badly placed to 'sell' their particular conception, even if it is well formulated (which it need not be), of a more

98

satisfactory relationship between the groups (workers—management—union) which have come into conflict. And there is no need to deny that 'power' may hold the balance until certain new legitimations are established.

Concluding comment: industry as a case study in social control

Factories, offices and other places where work is done are massively important parts of our lives, but they are in certain respects untypical. In a large measure the reason for their selection as the means to illustrate and advance themes in our discussion of social control is that certain aspects of solidary and legitimated relationships are brought out in extreme and consequently much more readily recognisable forms. Industrial organisation, even in spite of the impact of the growth in significance of trade unions, the varieties of legislation which prohibit for example, the employment of children and young people, restraints imposed on certain processes, factory inspection and the like, and a general climate of opinion that calls for greater freedom and democratisation of our institutions, remains intensely hierarchical and authoritarian. But one should not be too quick in finding a bogey-man or a bogey-process that is responsible for this. It is all too easy to maintain that this is a consequence of capitalism without making it at all clear what special features of the social system are being characterised by this term. All too often it turns out to be a shorthand symbol for a set of structures and effects that we disapprove of. Alternatively, and sometimes the two things have been confused (usually on the distinctly simplistic and really rather antisociological grounds that some group of individuals are so clever and powerful that they have virtually total control over the social process), the machinations of a few powerful people are blamed.

This is antisociological because it begs the question, so central to sociology, as to how much control we have over our social structures. Notice that it is very difficult to reconcile the ideas of a totally 'managed' social structure and of spontaneity and creativeness, unless one wants to confer the monopoly of these latter competences on the managers. Part of the preceding section of this chapter has shown how workpeople can refashion their interpretation of the world they live in, can amend, that is to say, the received ideas, the cultural aspect of their social reality. In this process old 'solidarities' come to be reshaped and new ones formed. This *in itself* constitutes change, for nothing can be quite the same as it was after this has happened. Nonetheless, and rightly, most people will want more than this; they will require some evident 'structural' difference in the new situation. In industry, this means not simply different management attitudes and reformulated or revamped justification for the old forms of authority relationship, it means a true refashioning of those relationships. It is here that the polemic against capitalism, understood as a system of management of the economy, may be appropriate, if it can be shown that this system imposes unwarranted constraints on the development of these new social structures.

But this brings us full circle to the legitimations of authority and the rational arrangement of purposeful social structures. Modern industrial societies are inevitably of immense complexity. As we saw in Ch. 2, 'solidarity' as the unique basis of such a society is hardly conceivable. The alternative is a legitimated structure, not something that is antagonistic to solidary structures, but at its best accommodates them. But *how* legitimation is achieved, and who, if any, are specially placed to influence legitimacy patterns, is the topic to which we must turn in the next chapter.

Social gatekeepers and labelling activity

Complexity is a matter of degree. To say, then, that the industrial realities which we considered in chapter 4 are of a limited and rather straightforward character when compared with total societies, while true should not be misunderstood. They are only relatively so and only so from a certain viewpoint.

If this is borne in mind, it can be useful to regard industry as having a boundary with the rest of the society. This has both cultural and structural aspects. The difference in complexity however, is fairly readily understood in terms of this boundary notion. We can readily see, for example, that certain activities are fairly clearly defined as 'work' activities. In terms of constructing a definition there would no doubt be some rather substantial problems to confront, but examples of boundary divisions are not difficult to find. For example, in day-to-day practice only a few people, who often regard themselves as rather fortunate in this respect, have significant difficulty in distinguishing their work from their leisure activity. The line between work and leisure constitutes *one* of the boundaries that distinguish industry from other institutional structures of the society. It is furthermore distinctly appropriate to regard industry as goal-seeking and functional, however objectionable terms such as this might prove in other contexts. Industry is functional in providing a variety of goods and services that are demanded within a society, however sensible or desirable and however created or stimulated such demands may be by the advertising media.

The principal goal of a good deal of industry, if not all, is that of making a profit on the commodities which they produce.

It in no way denies the detailed complexity of industry to maintain that it has a certain simplicity which makes it especially appropriate as the source of our social control examples. One can hardly *over*stress the way that wage work is massively taken for granted and institutionalised in our kind of society. Not only is the normative requirement to work for one's living hardly challenged, but the general form in which this is organised is not seriously challenged either.[1] The minorities—mostly gathered together under the general label of 'beatnik' in the public mind—who offer some challenge to this system of relationships have had only very marginal impact. As we saw in the examples, which were not purposely selected to this end, while it is fairly commonplace for dissent to be shown in industry to the point indeed where strike action takes place, the industrial organisation, as such, is only rarely challenged. The general structure of rule-making and rule-following is essentially taken for granted. Flexibility derives, rather, from established conceptions of 'reasonableness' and 'necessary give and take'. These are enough, most of the time, to take care of such accommodations as are necessary to ensure that the most natural sources of dissensus and change, the 'informal' or solidary groups in industry, are contained. Beyond this, one need not deny that there is a political struggle of a kind, which varies in intensity from place to place and time to time, under the impact of a very great number of variables. This political struggle in industry has its effects in changing the actual content and substance of give and take, and thus determines, to make further use of Gouldner's term, how 'indulgent' the 'indulgency pattern' will be. Nor need one deny, or should one forget, that sanctions are available to employers, the most powerful being that of the threat of loss of work and income. But this is quite clearly worked out within a larger framework, and even the sanctions just mentioned are not entirely arbitrary; not a simple manifestation of power.

A good deal clearly depends on what is regarded not only as 'reasonable' but also as plausible or realistic. This is a question of prevalent ideas, of culture. But there are structural concerns too which impose constraints on action in the interests of groups, associations and ways of life which may be threatened by disruption of other arrangements like that of industry. This is by no means a difficult point to grasp, but its general significance is perhaps less taken account of than it should be. The most obvious example, that of the family as a source of commitment, probably serves best in establishing the point that there are many situations which we will simply tolerate if we believe that a challenge will disrupt or endanger the solidary group. Concerns quite external to industry, such as our family relationships, play their part in the maintenance of the established organisation. Though industry has a clear boundary it has very clear links with wider society which provide both cultural and structural support for and constraints upon its system of control. And this clearly, is not a one-way process. In its turn, it is to be anticipated that industry influences other sectors of the society, promoting where it can the attitudes and social arrangements that suit it.

Within industry the questions as to who are the key figures seem simple. We will not be massively misled by looking at the chart which often appears in the company office purporting to show the chain of command. We are not misled because, although it tells a very partial story, such a chart indicates a rank order of people who have command over resources. This in industry means the authority to spend money, to hire and fire personnel, to initiate and amend policy and such like. We must tread warily on this but clearly, particularly in technologically very complex societies, it is not unreasonable to extend this idea to the society at large and to ask if there are groups in *key* positions in the social structure and if so, what is the nature of the control that they wield?

'Professionals' as gatekeepers[2]

The claim that 'professionals' occupy a distinct and important place in the social structure hardly seems contentious. By 'professional' we often mean a person with extensive specialised knowledge. 'Knowledge is power' is a very old adage indeed, so that a fairly natural piece of reasoning, consistent with the Durkheimian emphasis on the significance of the 'division of labour' in societies, is to regard the professional as a key figure. We shall see that it makes good sense in trying to understand some of the most general aspects of social control to ask some very serious questions about the significance of the professional in the process. But we must carefully avoid any tendency to regard the significance of the professional as self-evident or to exaggerate his social control function.

Part of the difficulty in connection with getting a proper perspective on the professional derives from two problems. The first is that of being clear on what basis we regard an occupation as a professional one. The second is that of avoiding the built-in conclusion that *only* professionals have such key positions and that consequently, thanks to something called a professional ethic, there is a benign resolution of what would constitute a distinctly difficult social problem. Some kinds of functionalist reasoning, we shall see, tend to issue in this last conclusion.

Among the most quoted and popular conceptions of what a profession *is* is that of Ernest Greenwood,[3] who suggested that professionals were occupational specialists who ranked highly on five distinct characteristics: (1) command of a systematic body of theoretical knowledge; (2) professional authority; (3) the sanction of the community; (4) a regulative code of ethics; and (5) the professional culture. It is worth while to consider these characteristics or attributes one at a time.

The command of a theoretical body of knowledge meets our first point. It provides a *necessary* basis for the occupational specialist to assume a special control position in the social structure. But it is interesting to consider the range of occupations that Greenwood excludes. Central among these is a group, not clearly codified, which is dependent on, for example, the job knowledge, rule-of-thumb information and skills possessed by craftsmen. Greenwood's stress is on long and arduous intellectual training as qualification for professional status. And this training is in what he regards as 'rational' knowledge. This, as we have seen in discussing Weber, is a difficult idea, but the major point Greenwood appears to be making is that it is codified and non-dogmatic knowledge.

This distinction has some curious effects. Among these are two distinctly strange cases of exclusion of certain occupations which may seem self-evidently to be professions in our normal understanding of the term. The exclusion of one of these may appear to suit our purposes rather well, but the exclusion of the other looks distinctly odd. The first of these is the Church ministry. This is odd because the priest is among the strongest candidates for the title of the 'original' professional. But the distinctly priestly knowledge, as distinct from the variety of specialised knowledge of psychology, sociology, and so on that he may acquire to help him fulfil what he sees as his social function is not 'rational' knowledge in the usual understanding of that term. It is certainly *not* scientific knowledge even if one were prepared to quibble about 'rational', and no priest would maintain that it was. The central tenets of religious faith are 'revealed', not scientifically discovered. In the strict sense of the word priestly knowledge *is* dogmatic knowledge, the knowledge of the creeds and beliefs of the faith and the implications of those beliefs. While it can be argued that Christianity especially is a rationalised religion in having worked out the internal logic of its belief system, even this does not make the workaday priest into the possessor of specialised rational knowledge. His distinctly religious acts are more nearly like a body of skills, the proper performance of ritual and ceremony. The academic profession associated with religion is that of the theologian, and Greenwood might wish to concede that it is the theologian that is properly regarded as the professional or as the source of professionalism. But this would be to move a long way from the normal conception of the clergy as professionals.

As was intimated the exclusion of the priest by means of these characteristics of professionalism might seem to serve our argument well. Given that our main concern is with society at the most general level it might seem very appropriate to maintain that although the priest *was* a key figure in our history and may still be so in other forms of society, he has now lost that pre-eminence. It is as well, however, to note the qualification carefully. At many levels below that of the total society the priest can clearly be very central. The striking feature about him, and this is an expression of the more general fashion in which the Church has operated as an instrument of social control, is that the priest can operate among the faithful both as interpreter and as controller. The nature of the commitment of the faithful is such as to provide the priest with powers to legitimate activities and to constitute a key figure in solidary groups where the emotional commitment serves more evidently than the rational demands. For the faithful the priest *defines* 'proper' modes of activity. We have, however, to concede this as the exception rather than the rule in modern industrial societies. This does not make the significance of the priesthood less important for the understanding of certain special groups and situations, and so perhaps very important for the understanding of certain conflict situations. Sectarian religious differences are all too familiar to us. The priesthood is now clearly a special case, both because of the predominantly secular nature of modern industrial society, and because of the wide divergences of religious belief and doctrine. Historically, the priesthood has been a central locus of social control; now it appears to be merely peripheral. But it is interesting to note its ability to 'define' situations when it is at the height of its powers.

Greenwood's required attribute of a profession does not seem to have caused a significant embarrassment in this case. The second example, however, creates a quite obviously more difficult problem. As Rueschemeyer[4] has pointed out, perhaps the two occupations most basically regarded as key professions in modern society are the medical and the legal professions. But while there is no arguing about the association of the modern medical profession with rational science the legal profession does not have the same form of relationship. Once again, while there is no denying the rational character of legal practice, it is not grounded in an empirical science. Most important for our purposes, we see that it is a normative, definitional kind of knowledge and practice with which the law is concerned. Empirical science has only a tangential association with the law, as with the need for the skills of the forensic scientist that are necessarily called on in some cases. Such skills are however, clearly peripheral to the main task of the legal system as a whole, which is with *judgment*. 'Rationality' is obviously involved here; there is no denying that judgment is, or ought to be a logical process, but it is not even a simple matter of logic for in a very real sense the body of case law established by the legal profession determines what the 'social logic' applied in the courts will be. On the basis of this reasoning there is no denying the importance of the legal profession, but there is clearly an embarrassment for Greenwood in fitting this paradigm 'profession' into the classification that his first professional attribute produces.

Greenwood's second attribute, *professional authority*, is

regarded as stemming from the first attribute of rational knowledge. Once again, it serves us to think of this particularly as the ability to define situations, but there is a further element: the ability to get things done, the legitimacy element. What we normally regard as professionals clearly differ greatly in this capacity. Greenwood has the doctor again centrally in mind and indeed gives the example of the phrase 'doctor's orders' as something which indicates the professional authority of the doctor. But this is specious, for even the doctor's 'orders' are not instructions, they are guidance and only in very special circumstances do they have the force of an instruction. We shall see later that the phrase 'doctor's orders' implies rather more perhaps than a phrase like 'plumber's orders' conveys; this is not the outcome of our greater competence to judge the plumber's skills, but much more significantly in the kind of social situations in which we seek a doctor's guidance. Part of the substance of this point resides in the fact that we may find it difficult to make a judgment of the value of the work or advice given by people with special bodies of knowledge and consequently have to confer a particular degree of trust in them. But notice the point that has been made here in speaking of 'plumber's orders': that the non-expert's dependence on competent and honest application of skills does not especially distinguish professionals, it applies to all but the most commonly held skills and knowledge.

If there is some truth to be conceded here we need to notice too that dependence on experts is relative. Industry and commerce make use of many experts, but this does not make industry and commerce dependent on particular professional experts. Unless they can be shown to have entered into some kind of conspiracy one 'expert' can be and often is employed to check the guidance and activities of another, either as a senior in the same field of expertise or in some other, possibly related, field. The relationship furthermore may not be apparent from the viewpoint of the expert himself, but be a functional connection seen from the position of higher management. The 'universal' controller in industry and commerce, the accountant, fits this role in his capacity as the guardian of cost-effectiveness, for however recondite the expert knowledge some measure of the financial return that this expertise achieves can usually be devised. Specialist knowledge then, confers authority only in a limited sense, and certainly does not provide a clear means by which to demarcate 'professional' from other kinds of occupation.

Greenwood's third proposed attribute of a profession is something he calls *sanction of the community*. This seems to mean a number of related things. In one sense it implies public confidence and its expression in certain kinds of reward; among these are such things as high status and deferential treatment. He also means a kind of public licence, something that he infers may be taken away if the privileged position that specialised knowledge confers is abused. But it is not merely a set of arrangements of an official kind and external to the professions which is at work here. Professions often set up their own controlling arrangements, in addition to having built-in certain attitudes to sound practice during the course of the specialist training. It is not Greenwood alone in the literature on professions who likes to make reference to an 'invisible college' of professional practitioners which is the supposed major influence in maintaining the appropriate professional standards. Professions are thus seen as being self-regulating in a very significant measure. The three main elements suggested by the 'sanction of the community' idea are thus a major degree of in-built socialised control over the practice of individual practitioners, 'absorbed' as part of the professional training.

Second, a further, associated means of control over individuals is their concern to maintain their reputation and advance their status among their professional colleagues. This may be supplemented by a variety of formal arrangements for 'disciplining' those who bring the profession into disrepute. Third, some broader state or public controls are envisaged, which guard the general public from the profession as a group. This is in many ways the most satisfactory of Greenwood's list of defining characteristics. Notably, however, this again applies most evidently to the paradigm 'professions' of law and medicine. There is distinct doubt whether a wide range of other occupations which claim professional status or are frequently regarded as 'professional' in an undefined way are under the control of these sanctions. While the many varieties of engineer for example have clear social responsibilities it is not a self-evident part of their training that special sensitivity to these responsibilities is promoted. Once again, the general social evaluation of competence, supported by the individual's need for the maintenance of self-esteem, is probably the significant safeguard against inadequate performance and malpractice, and this clearly has its influence on tradesmen, craftsmen and a wide variety of skills and competences not normally regarded as 'professional'. But the particular position of the medical and legal professions is again evident in considering the fourth of the attributes that Greenwood proposes.

The fourth attribute is that of a *regulative code of ethics*. The particular point that Greenwood appears to be making here is that what he wishes to call a profession is more self-conscious about its responsibilities, to the point where codes of conduct are actually set down. Professional ethics therefore are more explicit, systematic and binding. He goes so far as to maintain that the terms 'professional' and 'ethical' are synonymous in their application to occupational behaviour, so that in saying that a job undertaken by a craftsman or unskilled person was done professionally one is saying that it was done responsibly, ethically. Under this heading too he draws universal provision of the service according to need. The following composite quotation brings out his position on this.

A non-professional may withhold his services on such grounds [as age, income, politics, race, religion, sex and social status] without, or with minor censure; a professional cannot . . . the professional must, under all circumstances, give maximum calibre service. The non-professional can dilute the quality of his commodity or service to fit the pocket, to fit the size of the client's fee; not so the professional. Again, the professional must be prepared to render his services on request, even at the sacrifice of personal convenience.[5]

More evidently than at any time before in his account we become sensitive to what begins to appear as a loss of perspective, a shift to setting down some rules or advice for the ideal of a profession, as distinct from an account of the manner in which we may recognise a distinct subcategory of occupations.

The final attribute of a profession suggested by Greenwood is *professional culture*. This is extremely cloudy. What he seems to mean by this is something that is distinguishable as a way of life. He regards the individual professions as being subcultures which come under this more general professional culture. It includes a kind of 'calling', undertaking of the profession for altruistic motives, a devotion to good works.

We must pursue this question of professionalism a little further, with the aid of two other writers on the topic, but before doing so let us remind ourselves of the double aim in doing this. The first was that of determining whether there was a clear way of distinguishing some special kind of occupation called professional. We are in sight of a tentative conclusion on this. The second aim was that of determining whether there were any special persons or groups, professional or not, who could be regarded as having some rather special control function in the wider society.

Robert Merton,[6] who characterises professionals in a way compatible with that of Greenwood, enables us to get something of a new slant on both these questions. Merton provides a rather neater and more compact account of what a profession is which directly relates to the question of wider social significance. In his account he speaks of 'the concept of a profession' as being derived from a 'three-fold composition of social values'. These are the values placed on systematic knowledge and the intellect, on technical skill and trained capacity, and on service to others. The profession comes together in the service of these three commitments and so is essentially to be regarded as an altruistic form of highly skilled occupation in which there is a desire to formalise and systematise the skills. This is a neat formulation which outflanks some of the difficulties we found in Greenwood. In particular, as Merton specifically points out, it links the 'professions' with the centres of higher learning in the society. But, most important for our argument, not simply as the institutions through which the knowledge is to be acquired, but also as a device which protects both the professions and the society at large at one and the same time. This is done by the university acting as a kind of *gatekeeper*. It is the principal institution to function as the guardian of the professional and to act as the source of professional competences. It is in business, to use Merton's own terms 'to protect . . . against a swarm of near professions, quasi-professions and pseudo-professions . . . buzzing around to establish themselves as the real thing'. Notice that there is a curious tension between this mode of expression and what, if professions truly are to be regarded as institutionalised altruism, ought to be regarded as a very laudable ambition on the part of the 'quasi-professions and pseudo-professions'. But what seemed to constitute a problem for Greenwood is overcome with ease in this way of thinking, for the licence to professional status is conferred by the university.

What evidently cannot be denied is a spectrum of specialised skills the quality of which the layman has some difficulty in judging, at least in the short term. Perhaps more important than this, however, although this is not something that comes out with any force from our consideration of these writers on professions, is the ability of certain groups, whatever title they may be given, to *define* the appropriate quality of what they provide. This might give us cause for concern if our concerns did not seem to have been adequately taken care of by the range of self-denying ordinances that the functionalist account we have just studied maintains as the characteristic of professions. One need not deny that there may be 'something' even in the rather high-sounding talk of professionalism. In so far as these ideas of commitment and altruism come to be adopted by these occupational groups then certain self-constraints may be imposed. But we must recognise that what is being presented to us here is an account rather of an *ideology*, which we recall in another aspect is also a *legitimating* mechanism. So what these accounts appear to be giving us is not a vindication of the reality of professionalism so much as a comprehensive picture of how certain high status occupations would like society at large to regard them. These thinkers having discovered a potential problem of control have resolved it by offering a kind of ideal solution which appears to come about in an almost magical way.

The answer to our first question, then, is that it is useful to recognise the existence of a professional ideology, something that may be meaningful and significant because certain individuals or groups have come to adopt it. The extent of their adoption of the 'ideal', the degree to which this in practice effects their behaviour, what they regard as circumstances which relieve them of various of the self-imposed obligations, are all matters of empirical fact and have to be discovered by investigation. It is also useful to recognise the existence of certain 'positions' in the social structure where persons may be located in an important 'controlling' way. This we shall see, is true of small group formations as well as total societies, but we will consider the total society first.

Parsons gives a brilliant account of the special position of the medical practitioner in this regard. He first points out that there is a truly social element in health; fitness or lack of it is not *simply* a natural phenomenon. Among other things, sickness has a motivational element. Well-documented research indicates how individuals expose themselves in different degrees to the risk of injury or infection; in addition there are psychosomatic disorders and mental disorders for which there is no evident physiological cause. Illness is a possible way of responding to social pressures and of evading social responsibilities. Among the functions of the medical practitioner is the certification of illness, as a means of legitimating the patient's withdrawal from social responsibilities, taking into account the assumption that 'normally' the individual will work for his livelihood. The double-sided nature of this process is nicely brought out by Parsons:

> The legitimation of being sick enough to avoid obligations can not only be a right of the sick person but an obligation upon him. People are often resistant to admitting they are sick and it is not uncommon for others to tell them that they *ought* to stay in bed [emphasis in the original].[7]

Once certified by his doctor, the individual is both exempted from the responsibility of 'pulling himself together' and, at the same time defined as a person who 'must be taken care of'. Putting it in a way that Parsons himself might not entirely approve of, but which has been exploited by other writers, a dimension of the individual's freedom is thus relinquished. We can recognise here the substance of a half-truth that was conveyed by Greenwood's tendentious remark concerning 'doctor's orders', for certain benefits may be lost by the individual who evidently disobeys the advice of a medical practitioner when certified illness is concerned; that is when a justification has to be offered to others. Parsons sees a third element in the doctor's role as imposing an obligation to 'want to get well', both certification and help being given in a conditional way on this understanding. This is why 'doctor's orders' have the 'voluntary' element in them, they are offered as advice to the individual who 'genuinely wants to put himself right'.

From our viewpoint among the more fascinating and important matters brought out by Parsons's analysis is to highlight the fashion in which sickness though not normally regarded as such appears as a kind of 'deviance'. The function that the doctor is regarded as fulfilling, in addition to the evident one of restoring health, is a social control function in a variety of ways. In particular, there is the definitional role of being, with others in his profession, the agent who is absolutely central in determining at the most general level *what is to count* as illness. As part of an institutional complex, that is, the general practitioner can be seen as coming at the end of a chain in which he has an executive function to determine individual classification in terms of definitional criteria established elsewhere. Here the significance of the university and the various medical research institutes is once again established. This, as we shall see is not to be regarded as an entirely and exclusively *technical* competence and indeed the examples taken from Parsons of psychosomatic illness indicate how a doctor's skills must extend beyond a simple application of 'rational' knowledge. Parsons himself tries to avoid this implication. He maintains:

> The physician is not, by virtue of his modern role, a generalised 'wise man' or sage—though there is considerable folklore to that effect—but a specialist whose superiority to his fellows is confined to the specific sphere of his technical training and experience.[8]

But this qualification does not carry conviction, for the examples that he himself has offered already suggest that there is a significant area in which a 'filling of the gaps' in knowledge has to be undertaken. Once again, as with the previous discussions of professionalism, an ideal seems to have intruded on the untidiness of reality.

It is well to remind ourselves, as we have on previous occasions that many of these observations on social control operate at a number of different levels. This is brought out by considering the work of the French sociologists, H. Jamous and B. Peloille. In their analysis of changes in the

French university hospital system[9] they indicate the way in which senior practitioners resist the tendency for knowledge to become increasingly clear and rationalised, and consequently reducible to a routine. The interesting point arises here that professional practices are much concerned with areas of very *unclear* knowledge. This is no less striking in the medical field than in the legal where the form of presentation of a case, the 'job' knowledge of the attitudes and responses of various judges, and many other factors contrive to make the good advocate's skills more nearly like a subtle art of judgment than a clear matter of calculation from well understood if complex sets of interrelated natural scientific laws.

Jamous and Peloille, indeed, see how it has been of interest for certain groups to do their utmost to retain the ambiguous area of professional knowledge as a resource of particular value in the maintenance of old power hierarchies and the privileges which these provide for certain of the incumbents. In their case study this was achieved by defining clinical knowledge as the real basis on which the highest professional skills were acquired and then strictly controlling access to the patients by junior practitioners. The special characteristic of clinical knowledge is the ability to diagnose the uniqueness of each case. This is by comparison with the 'open' knowledge of the research institute, where the aim was to formulate clearly specified generalisations and to develop routine techniques. The resultant conflict indicates a vested interest in the maintenance of ambiguity on the part of the older practitioner, while the younger generation attempt to 'rationalise' knowledge. But Jamous and Peloille do not believe themselves simply to be establishing a point about a particular French situation or indeed offering a limited generalisation about power conflicts in the medical profession. Much more significantly for us, they are offering a definition of 'profession' in general as the particular groups of occupations at a particular historical period which can be characterised as having a high 'I/T ratio', as they put it. By this they mean occupations in which a high proportion of its recognised 'knowledge' has not been reduced to rules and techniques (T-technicality), but where there is a substantial degree of 'indeterminacy' (I).

Jamous and Peloille's study helps towards an understanding of control mechanisms at two levels, one internal and hierarchical, the other related to wider social structures. And the particular virtue of their approach has been to avoid the curious 'reassurance' which was provided by the other authors on professions whom we have considered. The doctor we have seen, on the basis of Parsons's reasoning, to have an important 'labelling' or 'certifying' function in the society, beyond but associated with the healing function performed for the individual. The 'reassurance' that comes from writers like Merton, Parsons, and Greenwood, however, flows in part from the seeming implication of their reasoning, which is not always easy to pin down but is probably related to certain common associations of the word 'professional' that we insist on carrying over now that society has somehow contrived to place these singular powers in appropriate hands. In Greenwood this kind of reassurance is further reinforced by the heavy emphasis on professional ethics, idealistic concerns and the internal controls exercised by professional associations. This is reassuring in spite of the rather hazy determination of what constitutes a profession within Greenwood's scheme. But not only is the notion of 'profession' not very well defined, but it is not clear that all those positions in which heavy social responsibilities fall on groups and individuals can be encompassed even within a very wide interpretation of professionalism. If professionalism is not generally recognised, then however significant the 'professional ideology' as a constraint on some occupations, it cannot be regarded as operative over those who neither carry the social esteem of professionalism or perhaps more important see *themselves* as having or aspiring to a professional status to which they regard these ethics as applying. It was always a dangerously

117

unspecified assertion that 'rationality' ensured the 'need' for certain key positions in the society, and that they, *uniquely* would be filled by professionals. Not only does the coming together of high skills *and* a particular social responsibility need to be demonstrated but so does the manner in which this 'social responsibility' is itself defined. In some accounts of professionalism, the 'professionals' appear to be offered not simply as the guardians of important structural positions in society but the only persons able to define the values that they will uphold.

'Ambiguity', and the related conception of 'lack of visibility' are the key notions that emerge from our consideration of this reasoning about 'professions'. There is no denying that specialised knowledge constitutes a kind of 'lack of visibility' for others and thus puts the specialist in a potential position of control. So with ambiguity; in a related way, whatever the status of their special skills or competences where there are areas of social life which are ill-defined, a potential control function is available to individuals or groups who are willing to define such situations. Association with widely recognised skills and knowledge may be the basis of their acceptance as the appropriate person to 'resolve' the problems. Alternatively, they may be so placed that there is indifference to the 'definition' undertaken or no general appreciation that there is any significant defining to be done. This latter is an aspect of 'visibility' especially related to a position in the social structure, and it is striking that no one would regard the position as being in the possession of someone placed there through the happy social logic which reserves positions of social significance for those with special knowledge. Even those who are so placed sometimes regard themselves as having 'sound common sense', rather than expert knowledge.

Illustrations: mental patients and 'skid-row' deviants
There is a great deal of powerful argument and some evidence

to suggest that mental illness, or a good deal of what is called mental illness, is misdescribed. This seems to serve a purpose of the resolution of certain interpersonal and social problems. It may not be the least satisfactory resolution for the person involved, but writers on the subject differ violently on this, with of course, all shades of view claiming the greatest concern for the 'patient', wrongly or rightly described.

Among the least strident and most rigorous of those who argue that 'mental illness' is a misdescription is Thomas Scheff, who writes:

> Mental illness may be more usefully considered a social status than a disease, since the symptoms of mental illness are vaguely defined and widely distributed, and the definition of behaviour as symptomatic of mental illness is usually dependent upon social rather than medical contingencies ... the status of the mental patient is ... an ascribed status.[10]

There is notably little argument among the well-informed in this field that psychiatric terms like 'schizophrenia' apply very vaguely to a wide range of symptoms. Consequently this constitutes one of those areas of social uncertainty open to labelling activity. Scheff and others concerned with this question of mental illness concentrate particularly on the power that these poorly understood 'ailments' bestow on the psychiatric specialist to certify and thus to incarcerate certain individuals rather than provide for voluntary treatment. A very poorly specified range of activities can be the basis on which effectively to remove the individual from society at large, or from particular groups, such as the family, who regard themselves as incommoded by the 'odd' activity of the 'patient'. It is important to stress this latter part, for as we have seen in another context this final 'labelling' function may be seen as the end of a chain of effects, so that 'labelling' is not simply happening at the most evident places or being prompted by the most evident powers or groups.

Scheff cites the work of Laing and Esterson[11] in showing that the 'oddness' of individuals ascribed as mentally ill can often seem distinctly rational and 'normal' when the context of their actions is known. In families the 'odd' behaviour often seems to be engaged in by the 'sane' ones when objectively considered and the 'disturbed' behaviour is of a pattern with that of the rest of the family. Clearly, they want to press the point that psychiatric disorder has a large social element in it and a rather small 'medical' one. Our point is a more general one. Whether properly regarded as medical symptoms or not, what we have here is a social control device and one that may work at a very great number of levels. It is especially interesting at the level of the family because its fundamentally solidary nature puts great pressures on the ultimate range of finally acceptable behaviour. The very 'closeness' and 'closed-ness' of the family relationship makes the definition of acceptable behaviour problematic, and the appeal to an 'outsider' a process full of tension. It is no accident that the viewpoint of the complainants rather than the 'patient' often prevail, for this commitment is no doubt recognised, even though it may be only intuitively. It is no accident either that, properly or not, the function of definition is performed by the medical profession for in our present society the medical profession performs virtually exclusively the role of 'outsider to whom one's troubles may be taken'. The division of labour between the priest and the doctor, that is, has been eroded.

Thomas Szasz, a more extreme exponent of the view that we have been considering also makes use of the connection that we have just noted between the decline of the Church as 'caretaker' of these disorders and the role of the mental health practitioner. In *The Manufacture of Madness* he argues, pursuing the theme of *The Myth of Mental Illness* that 'mental disorder' is a totally 'social' creation.[12] Extending the connection he argues that there is not merely a parallel but a direct relationship between the medieval persecution of witches and the present 'treatment' of those mental health patients who are officially certified. He argues indeed, that an extremely general form of social control is operating under either regime. Both witchcraft and mental illness provide for the necessary scapegoats in a society, those upon whom the evils of the system can be blamed. Just as witchcraft was a form of heresy against religious precepts, which were also the social precepts of the day, so mentally abnormal behaviour is the label given to unconventional behaviour in order to persecute it.

Szasz's arguments are powerful and should be read. Their relevance to our own concerns will be abundantly clear. But there is no doubt in the present writer's mind that he goes too far. His is no less a functional argument than the rather complacent arguments about the professions in society that we have considered. It turns that kind of functional complacency on its head, but nonetheless still argues from the premise that societies create institutions according to their 'needs'. In arguing that labelling activity is among the instruments of social control and that there are 'gatekeepers' in the social structure we want to avoid this conception. It may be true that the idea of 'mental illness' can be exploited by certain powerful groups in order to rid themselves of politically 'difficult' persons, but this insight is undermined by the notion of some kind of social 'inevitability'.

Egon Bittner brings home that labelling activity is not the prerogative of powerful persons or those of high status, or for that matter, evidently or distinctly under such persons' control. In a short article he brilliantly displays how the American police patrolman establishes a 'negotiated' relationship with the down-and-outs or 'skid-row' district inhabitants of two large American cities.[13] The patrolmen have to contrive a balance between their two official functions of 'law-enforcement' and 'peace-keeping'. Neither role is well defined, but together the roles are sometimes quite contradictory. Peace-keeping has to be achieved by establishing some form of accepted 'rough justice' among the down-and-outs. This means on occasions precisely *not* prosecuting some

121

offences, on others prosecuting on flimsy evidence or distinctly questionable grounds. A whole range of 'custom and
practice' develops and a relationship is established between
the patrolman and the down-and-outs on his beat that clearly
constitute a complex 'gate-keeping' process.

The case represents the situation of both ambiguity and
low visibility. There is no serious question of supervising the
patrolman's activities and clearly the 'cases' that do not find
their way to court are at least as important as those that do.
But it also serves social purposes to have these relationships
at arm's length. Broadly, the civic concern is simply to keep
the 'problem' under control.

'Gatekeeping' is by no means confined to high status
occupations with highly rationalised knowledge and skills, or
with special codes of moral practice to protect the 'customer'
or 'patient'. Nor need the gatekeepers be patently evident.

A note on the mass media

We have already had cause to speak of mass society, which
will also come up for further consideration in the next
chapter. The connection with the mass media seems evident
enough, but it is as well to attempt to avoid certain connotations, for while mass *society* is often used in a derogatory
way to imply unthinking, uninvolved, and often 'uncultured'
masses, the idea of a mass *medium* need mean no more than a
medium of communication that reaches large numbers of
people.

At some stage in reading this chapter it will probably have
occurred to the reader that the mass media have a distinctive
and perhaps the most central role to play in social labelling.
They perhaps provide a key institutional locus of social
control, a kind of central gatekeeper? It is difficult to sustain
this view. To some extent clearly, the political controls over
the mass media, and especially television, vary from one
country to another, being used in some as propaganda and

control devices. Even in extreme circumstances, however, the degree of effective indoctrination is doubtful. In less extreme circumstances who the controllers of the media truly are and what particular set of viewpoints they represent is an extremely complex and difficult question to resolve. Television in Britain is persistently attacked from many different angles as expressing some kind of bias, but the complaints are in significant measure contradictory and cancel each other out.

Among the plausible effects are the creation of a kind of penumbra of broadly accepted values, a very general commitment perhaps, in our society to democracy, tolerance and the like. Alternatively, it is sometimes argued that the media effects are almost entirely negative, the most profound effect probably being a massive desensitisation. In support of this view it is pointed out that fantasy violence, particularly the ritualised play portrayed in cowboy films and some other drama productions, often follows news film showing hideous atrocities. Fantasy and reality are thus said to become blurred and it is alleged that people become less sensitive than they might otherwise have been and consequently readier to accept what was previously unacceptable. The media may indeed have some such effect.

Much the most persuasive arguments against the simple indoctrination of us all, however, can be expressed in terms of the concept formulated by Elihu Katz, of a 'two-step flow' of communication.[14] It is maintained that the media output is used in a very selective way, that people employ it to bolster already firmly held opinions and attitudes. Much more important in the process of attitude formation are the influential persons and groups with whom we are associated.

This is a view that fits in rather neatly with our conception of the power of the solidary group and helps us, once again to link large-scale social structures to the smaller more familiar groupings of which we are a part. There is no significant inconsistency between this and the idea of the media having these very general influences. The likelihood is that they do provide a kind of weak support to certain very general values, those values which are so much a part of our way of life that in any case we rarely think to challenge them. Beyond this, when attitudes are to be transformed into actions, there would seem to be much more potent social forces.

Social control in mass societies 6

We have seen that legitimation and solidarity characterise the main forms of social control. Both operate at a very great number of interrelated levels, though solidary formations are more 'natural' as small-scale face-to-face formations and are 'fragile' as continuing social formations if they grow much beyond the scale in which there is frequent relationship between the persons who make them up. This is not to deny that a kind of solidarity can be established among the members of very much larger groups, such as trade unions and political affiliations. But there is something of a terminological problem here. The world 'solidarity' not only has a somewhat different meaning in these contexts but is itself an instrument of ideology and persuasion. Because it carries strong value overtones associated with the emotionality of the solidary relationship as we have described it, effectively to claim 'solidarity' for an organisation is to have people commit themselves to it, even if only at an intellectual level, *as if* it were the kind of small-scale relationship with its strong emotional ties that we have maintained as the paradigm case. This need not be entirely specious, for to the degree that persons come to regard themselves as 'alike', or sharing the same aim, or complementing each other, we have *one* of the bases of the solidary relationship. The paradox of this situation resides in the manner in which the relationship is intellectualised. It has become subject to justifications, legitimations and ideologies and is founded on them in a way that the basic solidary relationship we have been discussing is

125

not. The relationship becomes essentially cognitive rather than essentially affective.

This is not to express an antagonism to such social arrangements. On the contrary, in large-scale social structures (modern nation states for example), such formations may constitute the very life-blood of the society. They may perhaps best be regarded as secondary solidarity structures, by analogy with primary and secondary socialisation (see pp. 50—1) in recognition of the common factor that clearly connects them with primary solidary structures. This comes as a timely reminder that these relationships constitute a continuum and cannot be tidily separated out into extremes.

We need a further distinction, however, that will prove central to our final discussion of the nature of social control in mass societies. We need to distinguish the condition in which there is a real basis of choice from that in which there is not. Given certain totalitarian situations where both solidary and secondary solidary structures can be undermined and where communications channels can be closed to dissenting voices, a curious form of solidarity can no doubt be established. It is a solidarity that is founded on the basis of a lack of alternatives: culturally, because only a limited set of ideas is accessible; structurally, because only organisations and institutions serving the purpose of the ruling group are willingly permitted to exist. Some groups, because of their fundamentality or the countervailing power that they can wield can resist this and continue to exist, but measures may even be taken to undermine the primal solidary groups, like the family. This forced consensus has certain technical affinities to true solidarity which justify characterising it as *quasisolidarity*.

Community and association

In chapter 2 we gave some thought to the nature of a mass society, in considering with the aid of Durkheim's reasoning on solidarity the relationship of scale to social control. It was maintained that much of our day-to-day intercourse with others in such societies is in terms of almost pure instrumental role relationships. But behind these role relationships, we now see, is a great complex of taken-for-granted structural and cultural realities. The essence of these relationships was that the participants were without affective involvement and that they were distinctly predictable. But, as we have already noted, the *quality* of a society in which a very significant, if not the greater part of human existence is played out in activities in which the participants are indifferent to one another as persons and merely concerned with performance, might well be regarded as abysmal. It is distinctly dubious, indeed, on the basis of our earlier reasoning whether such a society could truly persist.

Durkheim's contemporary, Ferdinand Toennies, certainly regarded modern mass societies in this unfavourable way, though we shall see that this is not a view that Durkheim shared. In considering the nature of social control in mass societies we must look at Toennies's conception of the two possible forms, which relate well to our conception of simple and mass societies, and make a judgment as to the adequacy of his characterisation.

Toennies published his small but influential work, *Gemeinschaft und Gesellschaft*, in 1887.[1] Even his title causes us some difficulty. '*Gemeinschaft*' translates fairly neatly and revealingly into our term 'Community', in spite of being a difficult idea with all kinds of variation in usage. But, the alternative '*Gesellschaft*' can hardly be said to have an unequivocal English translation. 'Association' is the choice of C. H. Loomis, a distinguished American sociologist and translator into English of Toennies's book. But *Gesellschaft* can be and has been alternatively translated as 'society'. This is hardly as clearcut or as intellectually productive a tension as the tension between 'conscience' and 'consciousness' in Durkheim's thoughts, but it is interesting nonetheless.

127

Among the implications of the use of such a term is that (modern) 'societies' are 'mere' associations as distinct from the 'communities' of the past.

Toennies shared an evolutionary perspective with Durkheim and consequently saw *Gesellschaft*, which for the present we can understand as 'modern society', as a development out of the earlier *Gemeinschaft* pattern of human relations. There is little doubt that he regarded *Gesellschaft*-type society—in spite of his denials of this and his claim to be describing and giving an account of the necessary associated characteristics rather than evaluating the different types—as an altogether less worthy and satisfactory structure of human relationships than *Gemeinschaft* society. Because of this he is not unjustly regarded as a medievalist or ruralist, and differs profoundly from Durkheim, some of whose ideas were developed antagonistically to those of Toennies. This is the case, for example, with Durkheim's notions of 'organic' and 'mechanical', which we considered in connection with the notion of solidarity and which are virtually transposed as the terms given to ideas in Toennies, where 'organic' is the term used of *Gemeinschaft* societies as against Durkheim's use of the notion of organic solidarity in application to large-scale, 'modern' societies. And this, indeed, is one of the ways in which Durkheim stresses his quite different commitment to 'modern' as against 'earlier' societies. Most notably, the development of organic solidarity is, for Durkheim, the very basis of individualism and hence of freedom. It is associated too, as we saw, with a merely restitutive form of law, as against the harshly repressive law of 'mechanically' solidary groups where a kind of 'vengeance of society' is the practice. While Durkheim is intensely concerned as to the stability of the modern society—which, among other reasons is at risk due to the egoism that is a possible development out of the individualism that this kind of society makes possible—he is nonetheless committed to such a society. He does not share the rather sentimental attachment to 'community' that is evident in Toennies and indeed is also evidenced in a good deal of much more recent writing. This is a position which lends itself in vulgarised form to the support of 'blood and soil' doctrines and to certain kinds of anti-intellectualism. It is reasoning which can be the ideological instrument of the quasisolidarity recently mentioned.

It is clear from Toennies's writings that he was sensitive to the scale of human relationships we have already considered, but this and other factors were regarded by him as derivative. He regards, then, the 'forms of will'—natural will and rational will—to be the fundamental human foundations of the different forms of society. The second of these, rational will differs from the first in being deliberative and conscious and expresses itself in human social institutions, such as capitalism, in which society is constructed out of a set of essentially artificial devices contrived as the best means which the component individuals are able to devise in order to achieve the goals they have set themselves. From such a rational will the *Gesellschaft* form of society derives, a society particularly characterised by its suppression of emotion and what we might perhaps call 'spontaneity' in human relationships.

There is a certain fundamentality in the alternative 'natural will' which is characterised by an unreflective, uncalculating quality and, indeed selflessness. Toennies's chosen examples are the mother and child relationship and the relationship of true lovers. The society established from this intuitive, un-reflective type of relationship epitomises his *Gemeinschaft* type society. Toennies carefully makes the point that the natural will is not to be taken to exclude 'intellect' but distin-guishes what he regards as a 'natural' intellect from a 'rational' one. This is essentially an intellect of contrivance and artefact, a 'clever Dick' intellect unlike the former which is natural creativity. Once again, Toennies's examples are revealing: he compares the natural creativity of the artist with the 'artificial' intellectuality involved in manufacturing.

Toennies is able to retain the fundamentality of natural will by regarding *Gemeinschaft* and *Gesellschaft* as ideal—types, so that he does not anticipate that either form of society will be found in its pure form in the real world; 'natural' will or 'rational' will predominate in different social structures and at different historical periods. Our own kind of society in the judgment of most commentators would almost certainly have been classified as *Gesellschaft* (association) by Toennies.

A substantial quotation will provide a useful supplement to this summary, and also underline Toennies's commitment:

> The theory of the Gesellschaft deals with the artificial construction of an aggregate of human beings which superficially resembles the Gemeinschaft insofar as the individuals peacefully live and dwell together. However, in the Gemeinschaft they remain essentially united in spite of all separating factors, whereas in the Gesellschaft they are essentially separated in spite of all uniting factors. In the Gesellschaft as contrasted with the Gemeinschaft, we find no actions that can be derived from an a priori and necessarily existing unity; no actions therefore that manifest the will and the spirit of the unity even if performed by the individual; no actions which insofar as they are performed by the individual take place on behalf of those united with him.[2]

He goes on in this vein, further stressing the divisiveness of *Gesellschaft* society.

But was Toennies right in regarding *Gemeinschaft* society as some kind of virtuous ideal which we have lost with the coming of the urban industrial societies of our own time? Undoubtedly he was reacting in some measure to Marx's view that economics (some interpreters reduced this further, to technology) was the basic determinant of what societies are like. His reaction is to specify, as we have seen, not 'material' factors like the economic forms of production but a specified 'form of will', a kind of psychological determinant, as being the distinctive force which decides the character of a society. Modern practice is to regard these factors as subtly interwoven rather than one being more fundamental than the other.

At the descriptive level, however, the reader may be forgiven for believing that Toennies's *Gesellschaft* or 'association' form of society is a fair characterisation of mass society and fairly indicates the unsatisfactory nature of such societies and the true alternative to them. I shall argue that there is a middle term omitted by Toennies, and that we ought to regard community, association, and *commerce* as a better typology of societies. We shall see what this amounts to after completing further stages in the argument.

Mass society and pluralism

We have the beginnings of a conception of what a 'mass society' is like, but we have not considered an alternative, a pluralist society, which might well be regarded as an acceptable form of large-scale society. Durkheim's conception of a society characterised by organic solidarity based on a division of labour was something like this, though we shall continue to insist that it is better regarded as a blend of legitimation and solidarity, rather than a form of 'solidarity' proper.

A pluralist society is not difficult to characterise, though the judgment of whether a society is truly mass or pluralist is distinctly problematic. We can get a flavour of the contentiousness of the issues while obtaining a useful characterisation of both mass and pluralistic societies by considering a quotation from the work of C. Wright Mills, who was deeply concerned with the development of American society at the time of writing. For Mills a mass society is a society that has come under the domination of a power elite. Though it is not altogether clear whether this is cause or effect, it is a fragmented society; one in which true 'publics' have lost their power to influence affairs and have become opinion-takers as distinct from opinion-makers. He summarises the characteristics in the following very striking passage:

> [In] a mass [society], (1) far fewer people express opinions than
> receive them; for the community of publics becomes an abstract
> collection of individuals who receive impressions from the mass
> media. (2) The communications that prevail are so organised that it
> is difficult or impossible for the individual to answer back immedi-
> ately or with any effect. (3) The realisation of opinion in action is
> controlled by authorities who control the channels of such action.
> (4) The mass has no autonomy from institutions: on the contrary,
> agents of authorised institutions penetrate this mass, reducing any
> autonomy it may have in the formation of opinion by discussion.[3]

Let us attempt to 'read out' from this characterisation of
'mass society' what for Mills would constitute a 'pluralist'
one. It is clearly a society in which many different groupings
both *can* and *do* formulate and express opinions. This entails
that they form groups, for this is surely what must be understood from Mills's idea of a 'community of publics'. For this
to be effective he regards it as necessary that these groups
have access to the major means of communication. Beyond
this the groups must have the means to put their ideas into
action, which among other things involves access to funds
and other organisational prerequisites. But much the darkest
idea in Mills's conception of a mass society, and one in which
the positive freedoms that would constitute the alternative
are least evident, is the fourth. It is also the most interesting
part of the characterisation from our viewpoint. Mills seems
to be speaking of a kind of bureaucratisation of society, in
which the only activities of any significance can be carried on
under the watchful eyes and ears of 'official' opinion controllers. This has some affinity to our idea of 'gatekeepers' in
the social structure, and we will return to this.

There are certain stresses in the characterisation of mass
society which are probably overdone. Certainly, as our short
discussion of the mass media in chapter 5 indicates, Mills
probably overestimated the immediate significance of the
mass media as a direct means of persuasion. At the same time
there is insufficient stress on the media as devices for generating a general background legitimation for the society. The

intensely paradoxical nature of this will be clear. We are speaking of course of fundamentally cultural products, significant ideas; they are very general, conveyed often enough by what is left unsaid rather than by what is said but nonetheless 'cognitive'; that is, they constitute a basis of reasoning. Perhaps most important is that these legitimating ideas are capable of translation into a variety of 'forms of life', so that within limits rather different patterns of be-haviour are justified within the same general scheme. These depend on the significant groups to which we belong.

The flexibility of these ideas need not be regarded as terribly strange. For example, certain ideas about worthwhile activities must be regarded by one group as realistic ambi-tions while for another group they are simply a favoured fantasy. Groups can approve of certain ideas on quite dif-ferent grounds. Selective drawing from media images makes it possible to put together satisfactory combinations, so that in this latter case, dependent on the mood and the company, the favoured fantasy is not *too* unreal, but only a set of correct football scores, or 'a lucky run on the dogs', away. Clearly it is the solidary group that selects and 'gives life' to the available media ideas and legitimations.

Mills is thus wrong, except in perhaps possible but very unusual circumstances, in regarding media output as reaching only an 'abstract collection of individuals'. It normally reaches family groups rather than individuals, and ramifies with most people beyond this to a wide variety of solidary groups with some degree of selective and interpretative signifi-cance for the individual. What is missed in this is the possible solidary commitment to indifference to a great number of 'outside matters'. The solidary group, that is to say, has central significance in determining what is important or what is 'really important', and, not less significantly, what it makes sense to do anything about or to involve oneself in. Dad may be tolerated when 'holding forth' about the political news, but in much the same way that he is tolerated in holding forth about the local football team. He is no more expected to involve himself in politics than he is expected to ensure that the local football manager knows and takes cognisance of his views on team selection. If he does, he is by definition being 'difficult', 'odd', 'eccentric' or whatever, and will become subject to a variety of pressures for adjustment of both ideas and conduct. There are understood 'proper' and 'sensible' levels of involvement, which can of course shift over time, just as there are a wide spectrum of views on 'sensibleness' and 'proper involvement'; in part this is because multiple involvements and a variety of 'acceptable' interpretations are available in the society at large. As a possible instrument of a rather limited set of ideas constantly hammered home in a variety of ways, ideas that can constitute a cognitive background to these varieties of selective interpretation of events, the mass media are probably a potentially extremely powerful device. To put this more concretely, the media are probably the major instrument at the present time of the promotion of a complex of ideas that form the central legitimating basis of all relationships other than the fundamentally solidary ones: family, friendship groups, and possibly certain political and class formations. That legitimating base can be called efficiency oriented economism. It is much like the 'rationalism' that Weber saw as the dominating feature of modern societies. The principal thing that makes sense under this rubric is 'achieving aims efficiently'.

But it should be clear that this kind of media effect is not inconsistent with a certain kind of pluralism. It is a distinctly limited pluralism because the measure of all things outside the solidary relationships is 'efficiency'. In some measure even solidary relationships can become infused with this. This is unarguably a very significant constraint on the possible range of activities, but in my view it is not enough to constitute the claim that either 'mass' or 'totalitarian' society is the consequence.

A mass society need not be a totalitarian one, but Mills and others have regarded it as a distinct step on the way to such a society. Fundamentally missing, by comparison with the totalitarian societies with which we are familiar, is overt and evident coercion. But Mills was sensitive, though probably with not too sound cause, to the possibility of the avoidance of the most evident and overt techniques of coercion in the circumstances where an artificial consensus could be contrived. However exaggerated his fears, and in spite of the likelihood that his account of the manner of operation of the mass media and their effectiveness was probably defective, we should follow him, I believe, in recognising that direct and evident coercion is no longer the most important means of social control that a dominant group may exploit. This indeed is the reason why it has occupied so little of our attention. But it is worth a further passing comment.

What we normally call 'coercion' is simply the title given to immediately recognised and disapproved techniques. At the limit coercion may be regarded as any technique or device that constrains an individual and prevents him from doing (or thinking) what he would otherwise do (or think). All social control might thus be regarded as a form of coercion. But this would be misleading and particularly unhelpful in failing to discriminate in an interesting way. The trap we must avoid in discussing mass societies is the belief that the actually available range of true intellectual choices could be quite boundless and at the same time be tolerable. This is the fact that Durkheim saw so clearly, and is the cultural correlate of his conception of anomie, a condition in which individuals do not know what the 'rules of the game' are, do not know what to expect of the behaviour of others or what is expected of them. The condition of total intellectual uncertainty is almost certainly intolerable. In so far as a variety of agencies in the society establish a groundwork for anticipated and expected behaviour, therefore, a purpose is

135

being served that is not, in itself, sensibly to be regarded as 'coercive'. In speaking of coercion we are probably best served in confining the idea to the kinds of device catalogued for us by Moore in chapter 1, whose coercive status is evident. Evident coercion, it is true, poses a problem in our terms, which is the problem of the social conditions in which it becomes acceptable: broadly, how it can ever be legitimated. It can hardly be sufficiently stressed that this is not to underrate the social significance of coercion, it is simply to regard it as less sociologically interesting than the less evident devices of control.

There are two major causes for concern in Mills's image of mass society. The first we have commented on is portrayed in his fourth characteristic of mass society, where we have the image of a total interpenetrating bureaucracy infiltrating what would normally be solidary groups, primary or secondary. Mills probably had in mind the way in which agents of the party closely supervised the activities of those groups in Nazi Germany which were permitted a nominal independence. A more specific example might be the Soviet form of trade union organisation, a functional form of organisation which is not independent of the state. Alternatively, the syndicates of Fascist Italy, those curious mixtures of trade union and employer's organisation, were never more than 'showcase' institutions of debate and consultation, effectively subservient to Fascist control. It is clear that in our terms what are normally to be regarded as solidary organisations, the very source of pluralism in any useful sense of the term, the basis on which new ideas and activities might well be generated, have been exploited and undermined in the circumstances we have just exemplified. The basis of the exploitation resides in the fact that while they can be promoted as truly 'solidary' forms of organisation, conceptions of unity of purpose, brotherhood and such like can remain the grounds of social control. Explicit rational justification of the activities, consequently, is no longer demanded.

136

Effectively a *quasi*solidarity has been set up. Something indeed, that under fascist regimes there was an attempt to extend to the total society.[4] Notably, it was associated with a quite overt attack on rationalism, the use alternatively of a charismatic 'legitimation' in Weber's sense, and the promotion of a kind of father image, again associated with a solidary grouping, for the leader.

It is as well to stress that the primary solidary social formations are not beyond the destructive powers of certain kinds of regime and technique. Mills's fourth characteristic brings this out quite nicely too. During the Nazi period German families and friendship groups—the paradigm solidary groupings—were alike subject to the undermining influence of children and 'friends' who had come to regard their principal allegiance as owed to Führer and Party and consequently undermined the very basis of trust which is fundamental to such groups. But there was a second and rather different basis for a mass society that was expressed by Mills, a kind of decay of solidary institutions, predominantly, but not exclusively of a secondary kind. A number of authors have seen the relationship of this second kind of basis of mass society and the one that we have just explored as cause and effect, and something in which the mass medium of television and the family car have played a particular part. Let us consider this decline in numbers and intensity of the secondary solidary formations by looking at the work of Goldthorpe, Lockwood and colleagues.

'Affluent workers', instrumentalism and privatisation

The *Affluent Worker* studies, published only so short a time ago as 1968 have justly come to be regarded as classics in their field.[5] As is not uncommon with such work they have caused extensive dispute and debate. From our viewpoint the centrally important findings of these studies were of 'privatisation' and 'instrumentalism' among certain groups of

137

workers. These workers, it seemed had become almost exclusively family-centred. Hence the remark above, for their major sources of entertainment and recreation were those eminently family-centred recreations, the television and the family car. In this they were supposedly to be distinguished from both 'middle-class' and 'traditional working-class' groups, as being involved in very rich, and different, forms of association. The notable characteristic of the traditional working class was indeed the 'solidaristic' associations of which they were a part, while the middle classes formed important business and social groupings. Among the most important of the solidary associations for the traditional working-class group was their trade union, which was the expression of their deep commitment to one another as well as their means of protecting their standards of life and possibly enhancing them. The new 'affluent workers' which the Goldthorpe and Lockwood study portrayed, although normally members of their appropriate trade union, had a quite different relationship to it and to the other members. This relationship was characterised as 'instrumental'. The trade union was thus regarded *purely* as a means to serve personal ends, to provide wage increases, handle disputes with foremen and the like. It had become a functional organisation, involving as little self-involvement as membership of an insurance scheme might do. This typified all their activity, including their work which was regarded simply as the means to an end of maintaining a materially high standard of living for the family, and to which they were indifferent except in so far as it served that end. Goldthorpe and Lockwood were not concerned to argue that such 'affluent, instrumental, privatised workers' as these were becoming the normal or average type, though they seem quite often to have had this view attributed to them. There was some evidence, however, of the growth of groups without either the traditional working-class or middle-class affiliations, among them the so-called 'white-collar' workers who, although this is a very mixed category, are certainly among the growth sector in presentday industrial economies.

Clearly such workers as these could be the basis of a mass society. The 'other side' of the suppression of solidary grouping can readily be regarded as the growth of indifference to them, the unwillingness to form the kinds of association, with their solidary element, that seem such a significant part of a pluralist society. This could be rather close to Mills's conception of an 'abstract collection of individuals', although (as we have already maintained) it is family groups rather than individuals that constitute the 'isolated' units. But unless these kinds of association are suppressed or undermined this kind of fear is probably rather unreal. There are two good reasons for maintaining this. First, the extent of privatisation of the 'privatised' family is probably easy to exaggerate. When the privatised family get into their car at the weekend they do not always go sightseeing. They visit relatives and friends. What looks like an isolated group can rapidly be seen as ramifying into a complex web of relationships of a solidary kind. There is no reason to believe that these solidary groupings do not influence one another, or to regard them as having no significant ideas. They are not, as seems to be inferred, the inevitable foundation of unthinking consensus. Second, this reasoning ignores the basis of certain important kinds of solidary relationship, which may become rapidly established on the basis of *ad hoc* aims. Within months of the completion of the *Affluent Worker* studies, for example, the 'instrumental' workers there had discovered enough solidarity to enable a strike to be set up and sustained. Apparent privatisation does not inevitably undermine the ability or willingness of groups to come together for specific purposes.[6] Such events too can be the basis of new solidary groupings. Mills's concern notably, and perhaps almost too exclusively, was with 'commitment', with groups whose purposes were essentially political. It is as well to be somewhat concerned perhaps when the amount of significant

139

political involvement seems slight, but pluralism, it is well to remember, is not exclusively political pluralism, and the kind of political associations with which Mills was concerned are only solidary associations of a secondary kind.

Associations with political ends clearly demand some measure of solidary commitment, but the necessary measure may in fact be quite small. That minimal solidarity is achieved in recognising one's particular relationship with others in the pursuit of similar aims. Beyond this 'solidarity' may be specious.

Rationality and quasisolidarity

We can now return to our original comments on Toennies's conceptions of *Gemeinschaft* and *Gesellschaft*, and his evident commitment to *Gemeinschaft*. There is little doubt that the community and solidarity ideas carry a very strong emotional charge. I have conceded that solidarity is the basis of society; but that position must not be misunderstood, for this is to maintain on the one hand, simply that society can in the final analysis only usefully serve solidary relationships. Legitimated structures, in our terms, are devices for the achievement of ends, but the only ends finally worth serving are those generated from human interaction entered into and wanted for its own sake. This is one sense in which the solidary group is fundamental. Second, it is the final basis of evaluation of social structures; this is a simple corollary of the first point. This is why the solidary basis of social control is so important; it ramifies well beyond the immediate associations by establishing a wide range of commitments in the wider society which are regarded as providing a foundation for the immediate solidary commitments. The wider society is literally supported and maintained for the sake of the solidary groups. This fact can be exploited.

Clearly there are many social structures for which we should always demand an explicit rationale. Their justification can only be in terms of the service they give. But there is no virtue in not trying to order our affairs and refusing to set up institutional arrangements to serve those ends. This is where Toennies is wrong. There is no good reason for supposing that *Gemeinschaft* society would be undermined by reflecting on its relationships; changes might be induced, but it is wrong to regard a group as necessarily weakened by change and there is no particular merit in mindlessness. His proper target should rather have been equally mindless economism and technicism, production and 'efficiency' without social purpose, and this indeed is probably what *Gesellschaft* meant to him. It is this, the society that appears to have been 'taken over' by these kinds of commitment, the society in which the place for genuine solidary relationships has been reduced to a minimum, that I want to extend Toennies's typology to encompass under the idea of 'commerce'. This too is an ideal-type, fortunately not finally achievable. In it all relationships find their justification in 'legitimated' terms, in terms of their service to something else, even the husband—wife and the parent—child relationship. Given this, *Gesellschaft* society, translated as the 'society of pluralistic associations', can shed its negative evaluation. Both legitimated and solidary structures have their place, the puzzle is in the blend that is achieved.

The nature of quasisolidarity and its devices, by means of which in its most extreme form the totalitarian dictatorships may be constructed, will now I think have largely emerged. A clue to practices which indicate that such attempts are being made is in the abuse of solidary imagery. The imagery of paternalism and the family are clearly the strongest candidates, but ideas like 'brotherhood' clearly run these a close second. The clear aim when these terms are appropriated to apply to agencies like the state is to transfer the emotion that accompanies them. To make things more complicated they may not always be entirely specious. 'Comradeship', as the descriptive expression of a form of relationship that develops among men who face great dangers together and learn to value each other as individuals, is another term with these clearly solidary connotations. But quasisolidarity is clearly being aimed at, with the utility of the form of self-managing social control which it confers, when 'solidarity' is claimed as extending through the ranks of an army, so that a supposed link of this intimate kind extends from the 'humblest' private to the General Staff. It is only appropriate that in such cases the solidary commitment should apply in the most attenuated form. The significantly larger element in this sort of case and in our time is a legitimate justification in terms of function and efficiency.

Quasisolidarity, it is worth noting, can be the appropriate description of devices or attitudes applied to what are clearly secondary solidary organisations. The trade union, for example, brings together individuals at shop-floor level in industry with common supportive aims, backed by their concern with other primary solidary groups like the family, and is clearly a strongly secondary solidaristic organisation if it is to be appropriate to its function. Not much of this can sensibly carry over to such organisations as the TUC, which has to justify itself on legitimate grounds. Quasisolidarity operated in the Pilkington case considered in chapter 4, not as artifice or deceit but as a kind of misunderstanding of realistic possibilities. Consequently expectations and demands were made of this organisation which it could not conceivably meet. Its structure is rationalised round a very complex set of functions which have to be performed within an exceedingly demanding set of constraints. 'Our mate—Vic Feather' was an absurdly misplaced response. More appropriate would have been a questioning as to the range of legitimate responses open to such a body, and beyond that a judgment as to the likelihood of one response rather than another being selected.

This brings us to our concluding remarks and to an attempt to assess the measure of the individual's control of his destiny.

Social control and the individual

Sociological literature is replete with books and articles that tearfully announce the 'decline of community'.[7] It is even maintained that sociology itself is grounded in a conservative reaction to the industrial and political revolutions of the eighteenth and nineteenth centuries which destroyed essentially communital forms of society.[8] The past few pages have indicated the fashion in which this sentiment is grounded and offered a challenge as to its appropriateness. The sentiment is fundamentally reactionary in feeding on the desire and demand for a simpler social world. Of course, such a world is to be had if there is sufficient demand for it, but one should be sensitive as to the likely costs.

The curiosity of sociology is its need to be sensitive to what goes on in people's heads. It is clear that the world can be made very simple by providing simple images of it. Complete with scapegoats and ready sources of blame for the more blatant failures of the fantasy to be fulfilled this is what the Nazis provided in Germany: appeals to a mystical 'community' were among the strongest elements of their propaganda.

Although there can be little harm in promoting cooperative relationships, 'communities' (in the central sense with which we are concerned this means solidary groupings) develop and 'happen'. They are not creations and certainly not creations within some grand master plan of society. We have seen them as the natural bases of our allegiance. This is the fundamental difference between these relationships and the alternative 'legitimated' structures. But it has been necessary to put this relationship strongly into perspective, for to recognise the 'natural' qualities of the solidary relationship is *not* to regard it as the uniquely desirable social form. The proper response is not to regard formal structures as 'artificial' (except in the strict sense) and undesirable, and this applies even to the 'bureaucratic' form of organisation (other

143

than when, as with Crozier, the word is effectively being used to characterise some inefficient and unsatisfactory social structure). Such structures must be justified, and they are as good or as bad as their ability to satisfy us, as measured against these legitimations and the criteria we establish as the measure of their achievement. In a plural society we may not share either legitimations or criteria of judgment; this is one of the sources of tension, sometimes highly productive tension, in such a society. We have seen that one of the bases of resolution of the ambiguities that arise is resolved, either openly and overtly, or at some less evident level, by what I have called 'gatekeepers' in the social structure. Sometimes such gatekeepers are quite distinctly 'licensed' to perform this role; sometimes they are persons in positions of power who can exploit the ambiguities they discover; sometimes no doubt resolution is of an almost accidental kind.

Of the first of these—the official gatekeepers—we should be sensitive to the fact that their function often has ramifications of which we are only vaguely aware. The doctor constituted a good example for, *pace* Parsons, it is indeed precisely as a kind of generalised wiseman that the doctor often is used. Most evidently, a significant range of social decisions at the borderline of scientific knowledge, on what is to count as incapacitating illness (and possibly also a range of relativities regarding various groups or categories of persons in this regard) emerges from the practices of doctors. We may reasonably regard them as best fitted to perform this function; at the same time we need to be sensitive to the fact that it is not straightforward technical knowledge that is required, but that a set of social judgments is being made on our behalf. Social rationality should not become the handmaiden of technical competences by simple default.

But 'social rationality' is not itself a technology either so there are no evident 'proper persons' to fill these 'gatekeeper' functions. Where they are evident and regarded as significant they are filled in a variety of fashions in a pluralist society, consistent with the political pressures and influences that, at any given time, dominate. This is among the reasons for sociological sensitivity. The price of having a significant part in ordering affairs is precisely this sensitivity to the different bases of allegiance, the different modes of legitimation, and the different criteria of judgment brought to the situations that are of concern to us. Otherwise, the social order from our viewpoint is mere accident.

One of the earliest writers on social control, whom we have met, contended that one 'who learns why society is urging him into the strait and narrow will resist its pressure. One who sees clearly how he is controlled will thenceforth be emancipated.'[9] On the basis of our discussion we should find these remarks delightfully ingenuous. But we need have no quarrel with the sentiments that they express.

References and further reading

Some of the books cited are available in more than one edition. The particular edition used is indicated.

Chapter 1. The meaning and nature of social control

1. W. Buckley *Sociology and Modern Systems Theory*, Prentice-Hall 1967, p. 164. This book contains a very brief but interesting discussion of the concept of social control though one with which, as can be seen from the text, the present author disagrees in a fundamental way.
2. Thomas Hobbes, *Leviathan* (1651), ed. Michael Oakeshott (1951), Collier Books 1962.
3. T. Parsons, *The Structure of Social Action*, Free Press of Glencoe 1937; paperback edn 1968, pp. 87—94.
4. P. H. Landis, *Social Control*, Lippincott, rev. edn 1956, pp. 25—6. (Emphasis added.) This is among the best of the older, comprehensive books on social control; read critically there is still a great deal to be had from it. It is a distinctly committed book, with the author putting his faith in the educational process as the best means of attaining 'social control'.
5. E. A. Ross, *Social Control: a survey of the foundations of order* (1901); repr. The Press of Case Western Reserve University 1969, p. 51. Though long since outdated this book is of considerable interest to the historian of sociology for it was a pathbreaking attempt to establish the concept of social control as a key concept. The extract clearly reflects the tone of the book. There are some interesting short extracts in the second edition of Coser and Rosenberg's book of readings: *Sociological Theory*, Collier-Macmillan 1969.
6. B. Moore Jnr, *Social Origins of Dictatorship and Democracy*, Penguin University Books 1973, p. 486.

7. A. K. Cohen, *Deviance and Control*, Prentice-Hall 1966, p. 38. A compact interdisciplinary textbook with its major emphasis on deviance as the definition suggests.
8. T. Parsons, *The Social System*, Routledge and Kegan Paul 1951, p. 297.

Chapter 2. Scale of society: social control and solidarity

1. *Ways of Seeing* is the title of an interesting book by John Berger, based on his television series (BBC and Penguin 1972). It provides a useful illustration of the relativity and social functions of most art forms, and provides an interesting illustration of the point made here.
2. Max Weber, *The Theory of Social and Economic Organisation*, trans. A. M. Henderson and T. Parsons. Free Press of Glencoe 1947, p. 88. This is a translation of part of Weber's profound seminal work *Wirtschaft und Gesellschaft*, which remained uncompleted at his death. A three-volume translation, *Economy and Society*, edited by G. Roth and C. Wittich, published by Bedminster Press (New York) is now available, and portions of this and of some of his other work which was phenomenally extensive in scope are available in paperback editions. Among these in addition to the volume cited, are R. Bendix, *Max Weber: an intellectual portrait*, Methuen University Paperbacks 1966, and H. H. Gerth and C. W. Mills *From Max Weber. Essays in Sociology*, Routledge paperback 1970.
3. 'Convivial' is a term especially associated with Ivan Illich, who in recent writings has noted the minimal amount of easy friendliness that characterises the relationships in developed industrial societies. See for example, Illich, *Tools for conviviality*, Calder and Boyars 1973.
4. The distinction between culture and social structure made in this section is not unlike that made by A. L. Kroeber and T. Parsons in their short article 'The concepts of culture and of social system', *American Sociological Review* vol. 23 1958, pp. 582—3.
5. R. Firth, *Human Types*, Nelson, rev. edn 1956, p. 128.
6. See particularly E. E. Evans-Pritchard, *The Nuer*, Oxford, Clarendon Press 1940.
7. Emile Durkheim's *The Division of Labour in Society* is, with *Suicide, The Elementary Forms of the Religious Life* and the short methodological treatise *The Rules of Sociological Method*, among the most important of his work. Durkheim shares the distinction

with Weber of being the most influential of the sociological writers of the later part of the nineteenth century and early part of the twentieth. The only figure currently regarded as of comparable stature is Karl Marx who, of course, belongs to an earlier generation of thinkers. These volumes are now available in paperback editions: *The Elementary Forms of the Religious Life*, trans. J. W. Swain, Allen and Unwin 1915; *The Rules of Sociological Method*, trans. S. A. Solovay and J. H. Mueller, 8th edn, Free Press of Glencoe 1938; *The Division of Labour in Society*, trans. G. Simpson, Free Press of Glencoe 1964.

8. Durkheim, *The Division of Labour in Society*, p. 40.
9. *Ibid.*, p. 50. The setting of this remark indicates that it was intended polemically and ironically. Durkheim's target was a use of 'civilisation' which referred to merely technical 'advances'. Durkheim wishes to maintain that the division of labour also has *moral* significance.
10. *Ibid.*, p. 56.
11. *Ibid.*, p. 69.
12. *Ibid.*, pp. 105—6.
13. *Ibid.*, p. 127.
14. *Ibid.*, p. 130.
15. The concept of 'community' like so many others in our field of concern has a wide range of applications. The reader might like to consult D. Minar and S. Greer, *The Concept of Community* (Aldine 1969) to develop an understanding of the multiplicity of uses beyond the necessarily short discussion possible here.

Chapter 3. Social control: socialisation and legitimacy

1. E. Leach, 'A runaway world?', Reith Lectures 1967, *The Listener* 30 Nov. 1967, p. 685.
2. The term is especially associated with G. H. Mead, an American psychologist and philosopher who has been extremely influential, especially as the founder of a technique of sociological investigation called 'symbolic interactionism'. His great influence was as a teacher and an important selection of his lectures has been edited and compiled by C. W. Morris in the volume *Mind, Self and Society*, University of Chicago Press 1968.
3. D. Wrong, 'The oversocialised conception of man in modern sociology'. Originally published in the *American Sociological Review*, vol. 26, this important article will be more readily avail-

able to the average reader in the Coser and Rosenberg volume cited above (ch. 1, n5); the quotation is from the third edition, p. 125.
4. For a clear, concise account of the Marxist conception of capitalist society it is still hardly possible to better *The Communist Manifesto*, written by Marx and Engels themselves.
5. For Weber's own account of the notion of legitimacy see especially pp. 124–32 and pp. 324–63 of *The Theory of Social and Economic Organisation* (see ch. 2, n. 2).
6. For Weber's account of bureaucracy see pp. 329–41 in *The Theory of Social and Economic Organisation* and chapter 8 of *From Max Weber; essays in sociology* (see ch. 2, n. 2). For recent discussions of the concept see M. Albrow, *Bureaucracy*, Macmillan 1970, and D. Warwick, *Bureaucracy*, Longman 1974 (uniform with the present volume).

Chapter 4. An illustration: social control in industry

1. A. W. Gouldner, *Wildcat Strike*, Harper Torchbooks 1954.
2. Max Weber, *The Protestant Ethic and the Spirit of Capitalism*, trans. T. Parsons, Unwin University Books 1930.
3. R. Bendix, *Work and Authority in Industry*, Wiley 1956.
4. The definitive report of the research is in F. J. Roethlisberger and W. J. Dickson, *Management and the Worker*, Harvard University Press 1949. There are good short accounts in J. Madge, *The Origins of Scientific Sociology*, Tavistock 1970, ch. 6, and G. C. Homans, *The Human Group*, Routledge 1951, ch. 3. The reader may also like to compare Homans's notion of social control, elaborated in ch. 11, with the present author's approach.
5. A useful short introduction to Taylor's thought is available in A. Tillet, T. Kempner and G. Wills, *Management Thinkers*, Penguin 1970.
6. The interesting ideas of 'unitary' and 'pluralistic' relationships in industry are developed by A. Fox in Royal Commission on Trade Unions and Employers' Associations (Donovan Commission), Research Paper No. 3, 'Industrial sociology and industrial relations', HMSO 1966.
7. T. Lupton, *On the Shop Floor*, Pergamon 1963.
8. *Ibid.*, pp. 182–3.
9. *Ibid.*, p. 2.
10. *Ibid.*, p. 195.

11. M. Crozier, *The Bureaucratic Phenomenon*, Tavistock 1964.
12. *Ibid.*, p. 153. (Emphasis added.)
13. Albrow: see ch. 3, n. 6.
14. Crozier, *The Bureaucratic Phenomenon*, p. 151.
15. A. W. Gouldner, *Wildcat Strike*, Harper Torchbooks 1954 and *Patterns of Industrial Bureaucracy*, Free Press of Glencoe 1954.
16. *Wildcat Strike*, p. 26.
17. T. Lane and K. Roberts, *Strike at Pilkingtons*, Collins/Fontana 1971.
18. *Ibid.*, p. 188. (The earlier emphasis has been added.)
19. *Ibid.*, p. 139.

Chapter 5. Social gatekeepers and labelling activity

1. So, for instance, H. Beynon's recent book, *Working for Ford* (Allen Lane 1973), records how workers attempt to establish control over the speed of the conveyor belts which determine the pace at which they must work, but even the most radical of them have quite limited ambitions with regard to taking over what are regarded as managerial 'prerogatives'.
2. One of the earliest uses of this idea seems to have been that of Kurt Lewin who, in undertaking some wartime research discovered certain 'influentials' to whom messages were most usefully directed in order to have maximum effect.
3. E. Greenwood, 'Attributes of a profession', *Social Work* 2 (July 1957), 45—55. Greenwood's article is reprinted in H. M. Vollmer and D. L. Mills reader, *Professionalization*, Prentice-Hall 1966.
4. D. Rueschemeyer, 'Doctors and lawyers: a comment on the theory of the professions', *Canadian Review of Anthropology and Sociology*, Feb. 1964, pp. 17—30.
5. Greenwood *op. cit.*, p. 15 in the Vollmer and Mills volume.
6. R. K. Merton, *Some Thoughts on the Professions in American Society*, Brown University Papers (Providence R.I.) No. 37, 1960.
7. T. Parsons, *The Social System*, pp. 436—7.
8. *Ibid.*, p. 435.
9. H. Jamous and B. Peloille, 'Professions or self-perpetuating systems? Changes in the French university hospital system', in J. A. Jackson, ed., *Professions and Professionalization*, Cambridge University Press 1970, ch. 4.
10. T. J. Scheff, *Being Mentally Ill*, Weidenfeld and Nicolson 1966, pp. 128—9. For those readers with access to a university library a

concise formulation of Scheff's theory is available in *Sociometry*
26 (1963), pp. 436—53.

11. In particular, R. D. Laing and A. Esterson, *Sanity, Madness and the Family*, Penguin 1970.
12. T. S. Szasz, *The Myth of Mental Illness*, Hoeber-Harper 1961, and *The Manufacture of Madness*, Routledge 1971.
13. E. Bittner, 'The police on "skid-row": a study of peace keeping', *American Sociological Review*, 32, No. 5 (Oct. 1967), 699—715.
14. E. Katz and P. F. Lazarsfeld, *Personal Influence*, Free Press of Glencoe 1955.

Chapter 6. Social control in mass societies

1. Ferdinand Toennies, *Community and Association*, trans. C. P. Loomis, Routledge 1955.
2. *Ibid.*, p. 74.
3. C. W. Mills, *The Power Elite*, Oxford University Press 1956, p. 304 and ch. 13, *passim*. For a useful summary analysis of the different sources of 'Mass society' reasoning see also W. Kornhauser, *The Politics of Mass Society*, Routledge 1960.
4. There is a massive literature on Fascism. Of its manifestation in the National Socialism of Hitler's Germany the present writer found R. Grunberger, *A Social History of The Third Reich* (Weidenfeld and Nicolson 1971) particularly interesting and helpful.
5. J. H. Goldthorpe, D. Lockwood, F. Bechhofer and J. Platt, *The Affluent Worker*, 3 vols, 1. *Industrial Attitudes and Behaviour*; 2. *Political Attitudes and Behaviour*; 3. *The Affluent Worker in the Class Structure*, Cambridge University Press 1968—69.
6. W. W. Daniel has argued strongly that workers' responses are strongly conditioned by circumstances and that this point has been missed in the *Affluent Worker* studies. See 'Understanding employer behaviour in its context: . . .', in John Child, ed., *Man and Organisation*, Allen and Unwin 1973.
7. M. Stein's, *The Eclipse of Community*, Princeton University Press 1960; paperback Harper and Row, is in this vein, though it does also contain some very useful summaries of American community studies.
8. This thesis is particularly associated with R. Nisbet and expounded in his popular book on the history of sociological ideas, *The Sociological Tradition*, Heinemann 1967.
9. Ross, *op. cit.*, p. 441.

Index

Index

socialisation, 4—6, 48—56
  universality of, 51—3
sociological problem and social
  problem, distinguished, 21
solidarity, 27, 34, 40—6, 48—56,
  68, 81, 88—90, 94—5, 98,
  125, 133, 136, 138—42
Spanish Inquisition, 18
Stein, M., 151
Szasz, T., 120—1

Taylor, F. W., 78, 80—1
Tillet, A., 149
Toennies, F., 46, 127—31,
  140—1

totalitarian society, 126, 134—7,
  141, 143

United Nations Organisation, 46
'unsocialised' behaviour, 52—3

values, defined, 5

Warwick, D., 149
Weber, M., 22—3, 29, 44, 56—9,
  62, 64, 66—7, 69—70, 85,
  87, 92, 134
'wildcat' strike, 90
Willis, G., 149
work ethic, 70—2
Wrong, D., 54—5

The key concepts for the understanding of the complex process of social control are, the author argues, those of 'solidarity' and 'legitimation'. Making use of classical writings he illustrates how the relationship of the complex of processes captured by these fundamental notions is the key to understanding much that is puzzling as to the nature of social order.

There is a careful exposition of how other key ideas in sociology relate to those of solidarity and legitimation. In particular, solidarity is associated with the socialization process and is most closely related to our informal, emotionally-grounded relationships to others. Legitimation, however, is much more nearly related to the power phenomena in society and to the devices for promoting attitudes and ideas. Societies and groups have 'key positions' which are of central importance in maintaining certain basic social relationships. But these key positions and the manner in which they operate are by no means, as the text shows, self-evident.

Using industry as an illustration, the manner in which solidary groups with their commitments relate to and interact with formal, legitimated social structures is revealed and social order is seen as a very complex, 'emergent' process. This approach to social control consequently avoids the bias evident in more static conceptions of social control, in which 'order' is understood as consensus and non-conformity of all kinds is relegated to a residual category of 'deviance.'

The final chapter brings home the distinct social relevance of the discussion. The major social implication of the discussion is that while we may not be masters of the societies in which we live in the sense of having the means to mould them to our desires, sociological reasoning at least reveals certain dangers which may be avoidable. So rational, legitimated social structures and solidary social relationships each have their proper place in a society, but great dangers exist in the possible misplaced adoption of attitudes and techniques appropriate to one rather than the other.